Hua Hu Ching

HUA HU CHING

The Later Teachings of *Lao Tzu*

Hua-Ching Ni

Shambhala
Boston & London
1995

Shambhala Publications, Inc.
Horticultural Hall
300 Massachusetts Avenue
Boston, Massachusetts 02115
www.shambhala.com

© 1979, 1995 by Hua-Ching Ni

First published by SevenStar Communications as part of the volume
The Complete Works of Lao Tzu by Hua-Ching Ni.

Printed in the United States of America

Distributed in the United States by Random House, Inc.,
and in Canada by Random House of Canada Ltd

LIBRARY OF CONGRESS CATALOGING-IN-PUBLICATION DATA

Ni, Hua-Ching.
    Hua hu ching: the later teachings of Lao Tzu/Hua-Ching Ni.—1st ed.
        p.   cm.
    ISBN 1-57062-079-2 (acid-free paper)
    1. Wang, Fu, 4th cent.   Lao-tzu hua hu ching.   2. Taoism.   I. Wang, Fu,
    4th cent.   Lao-tzu hua hu ching.   English.   1995.   II. Title.
B11900.W345N5   1995   94-36153
299'.51482—dc20   CIP
BVG 01

This book is dedicated to those who cherish a broad spiritual attitude and appreciate the wisdom of natural inspiration in giving the light of perpetual value to guide all people of all generations.

Contents

Contents

Preface

This book is intended to present information and techniques that have been in use throughout the Orient for many years. This information and these practices utilize a natural system within the body; however, no claims are made regarding their effectiveness. The information offered is to the author's best knowledge and experience and is to be used by the reader at his or her own discretion and liability.

Because of the sophisticated nature of the information contained within this book, it is recommended that the reader also study the author's other books for a broader understanding of energy-conducting exercises and a healthy lifestyle.

People's lives have different conditions, and their growth has different stages. Because the background of people's development cannot be unified, there is no single practice that can be universally applied to everyone. Thus, it must be through the discernment of the reader that the practices are selected. The adoption and application of the material offered in this book must therefore be the reader's own responsibility.

The author and publisher of this book are not responsible in any manner for any harm that may occur through following the instructions in this book.

According to the teaching of the Universal Way, male and female are equally important in the natural sphere. This fact is confirmed in the diagram of Tai Chi. Thus, discrimination is not practiced in our tradition. All my work is dedicated to both genders of the human race.

Wherever possible, constructions using masculine pronouns to represent both sexes are avoided; where they occur, we ask your tolerance and spiritual understanding. We hope that you will take the essence of my teaching and overlook the superficiality of language. Gender discrimination is inherent in English; ancient Chinese pronouns do not have differences of gender. I wish for all of your achievement above the level of language or gender.

Introduction

Lao Tzu's *Tao Te Ching* is one of the most cherished and frequently translated works in the world. Its pages contain the simple yet most profound truths of the universe. Taoists consider Lao Tzu to be the greatest teacher of all times and have given him the spiritual title "Most Exalted One." He is regarded as a sage of high heavenly energy, and legend states that he spent eighty-one years in his mother's womb. In plain language this means that it took many years for him to bear the fruit of wisdom.

As the emperor's librarian and keeper of the Royal Archives, Lao Tzu came into contact with the wisdom and knowledge of China's greatest sages before the time of the Yellow Emperor (2697 BCE). As time passed, he became aware that a time of great confusion and spiritual disintegration was to befall the empire. He decided to leave society and live a life of seclusion that was in harmony with nature. Thus he rode westward on the back of a water buffalo. When he came to the Han Gu Pass at the border of China, he was requested by the pass official to write down the essence of his wisdom. This classic has since been called the *Tao Te Ching*.

Many people are familiar with this story; however, few are aware that, as Lao Tzu traveled on, he continued to share his teachings with those who sincerely sought to live according to the Universal Way. Only one known compilation of those later teachings, known as the *Hua Hu Ching,* has survived.

During the Yuan dynasty, the emperor Shuen Ti (r.1333–1367 CE) was swayed by the jealous and prejudiced religious leaders of that time to ban the *Hua Hu Ching* because many associated him with the prince who appears as Lao Tzu's student in the book. The influence of the book can be seen in the later teachings of the Buddha, as well as in the teachings of Sufism. The Ch'an school of Chinese Buddhism and Zen Buddhism in Japan are actually ancient Taoist teachings wearing a new garment.

The *Hua Hu Ching* is a very rare manuscript and even appeared in a number of different versions in early China. Few, if any, complete and accurate copies of this work exist today. It is only through the oral transmission of the teachings contained in the *Hua Hu Ching* through generation after generation of Taoist masters that the teaching has been preserved intact. This is my own version, which represents the end of the cultural race between southern and northern Asia. The integration of the teachings brought the sensitive mind of the southern people to meet the natural focus of the early developed teachers of northern Asia. When my universal mind reaches still deeper than the universal mind of Lao Tzu, it is hoped that new progress will be made.

Historically, scholars still wonder whether an individual called Lao Tzu existed, or whether Lao Tzu's book was only the work of the pass official after being inspired by a dignified traveler. It is the same with the story of Genesis, the story of Abraham, the experience of Moses and the teaching of Jesus. No one wrote them down until years or centuries later. In modern times, the copyright is respected because the genuine author gives his or her name, but Fu Shi, Lao Tzu, Shakyamuni, and the cultural leaders of all places could not really insist upon genuine individual authority. This means that cultural differences do not exist, although a mind that lacks development could hold on to a certain stage of expression as the truth of all time.

The teachings of Lao Tzu are both rational and miraculous. They appear to be like a cup of clear, fresh water, yet their subtle power is immeasurable. They are the expression of utmost simplicity and purest wisdom. They enable people at all different levels of development to partake of this wisdom, just as pure water refreshes and supports all aspects of life. Many, however, are unable to accept this miraculous power because these unadorned teachings do not arouse their imagination or stimulate their illusions. If these teachings did this, however, they would merely be another impediment to true inner growth.

Truth itself is power. Through persistent study of this book, many kinds of help can be produced. Many recorded anecdotes reveal another realm of life that is pointed to in the teachings of Lao Tzu. The shell of a book can be burned by those who have not attained any spiritual development, but there is no one who can damage the universal mind. For this reason, this precious book is now in your hands.

Hua Hu Ching

~· 1 ·~

There once was a great white-bearded master who appeared at the boundary of the Central Territory* on his journey west. Followers came from everywhere to sit at his feet, for he was a model of universal harmony. His teaching was so simple, yet so profound. His instruction was neither ordinary religion nor worldly wisdom, yet it revealed the truth of every aspect of the universe. All of his friends and followers lived virtuously and performed whatever work came to them joyfully. They maintained a peaceful, righteous way of life and enjoyed the abundance of their being. After their daily work was completed, they cleansed themselves carefully and fed themselves properly. Then they went to the garden where the old master stayed and awaited his precious instruction.

~· 2 ·~

On the occasion of one such gathering, a wise disciple who was the prince of the country rose among the group and humbly saluted the master, saying, "Venerable master of the world, one who is virtuous without discrimina-

---

*In ancient times, this term was used to refer to the country that is known as China today.

tion takes care of those who practice virtue and selflessness. One who is virtuous without discrimination also guides those who do not practice virtue and selflessness. Please instruct us. How should men and women who are motivated to attain the correct awareness of their true nature calm their minds? What path should they follow in order to attune their minds harmoniously to all aspects of life?"

The old master said, "Well, well, one of virtue and wholeness takes care of those who practice virtue and selflessness. One of virtue and wholeness also guides those who do not practice virtue and selflessness, as you said.

"Please listen well. Any good person who is motivated to attain awareness of the whole truth should follow the Universal Way to calm his mind and harmonize it with all aspects of life."

The prince said gladly, "Most Venerable Master, we are ready to receive your precious guidance with great joy."

⌣· 3 ·⌐

The master told the prince and all the followers, "All of my friends and disciples should attune their minds to all life and hold no antagonism toward any living thing whether it be born of womb, egg, moisture, or any other kind of transformation; whether it can think or is unable to think; whether it has form or is formless. You should dissolve all discrimination of individuality and absorb all things into a harmonious oneness.

"The virtue of a highly evolved being embraces all people and things and dispels the darkness which isolates them. Although numberless lives are illuminated, one who is unaware of the whole really helps no one. Why is this so? Kind prince, if one still holds the divisive mental concepts of self and others, male and female, longevity and brevity, life and death, and so on without end, then one does not have an all-embracing awareness."

⌣· 4 ·⌣

The master continued, "One who practices virtue and selflessness should not hold any particular idea in his mind about how to fulfill his virtue, for virtue is the very nature of one's being. One should always be willing to assist others selflessly and unconditionally by offering one's skills and achievements to serve them. One should be willing to give away the things one cherishes most and even offer one's life to assist others.

"One should not restrict one's service by making distinctions based on color, nationality, family or social relationships, sensory perceptions, or any other relative conditions. To restrict the ways in which one would render service to others in order to suit one's personal preference is potentially harmful.

"Kind prince, if one relates to others and serves them only according to his own design, it is as if he had entered darkness and was blind. He might help some people by chance and he might also injure some. But, if one does not limit oneself by imposing special terms on his service, then he is like a person with good vision who sees clearly and whose influence is purely positive.

"Following the Universal Way means practicing selflessness and extending virtue to the world unconditionally. In this way one not only eliminates the heavy contamination accumulated throughout many lifetimes, but may also bring about the possibility of restoring one's original divine nature and become an integral being of the multi-universe. This is the only way to dissolve the self-created agony, misery, and tragedy that are experienced in one's life.

"Every expression of life is the reality of life. One's every movement and activity evoke a response from the subtle energy of the universe. When one does not limit himself by imposing conditions on rendering service to others, the blessings evoked will also be limitless."

～5～

The old master said, "Kind prince, what do you think? Can the great space of the East be measured by the mind?"

The prince replied, "No, Venerable Teacher."

"Kind prince, what do you think? Can the space of the four directions, as well as above and below, which constitute the profound vastness of the universe, be measured by the mind?"

"No, Venerable Teacher."

"Kind prince, the mind is just as immeasurable as the vast universe. An integral being settles his mind just as the vast universe settles itself. He unites his mind with the unnamable Subtle Origin of the multi-universe in which there is no past, present, or future. This is how an integral being deals with his mind."

⌣· 6 ·⌢

"Kind prince," asked the old master, "what do you think? Can the subtle cosmic body of the Integral One be seen in any beautiful form?"

"No, Venerable Teacher," replied the prince, "the subtle cosmic body of the Integral One cannot be seen in any beautiful form because to the Integral One there is nothing which can be considered as form."

"Kind prince, as soon as the Integral One is mentioned people immediately formulate images of it in their imaginations. Then they try to make the reality of it conform to their imaginary concept of it. The Integral One is truly imageless, yet in the attempt to make it conform to an image, people distort its reality and separate themselves from it."

The prince inquired of the master, "Venerable Teacher, will there be people in the future who will have the opportunity to learn and follow the Universal Way of Life by studying these bamboo scrolls on which your great teachings are recorded?"

The master told him, "Kind prince, please do not wonder about this. After I depart, even many, many generations later, if there are still people who seek the Universal Way, they will receive this precious guidance.

"Those who seek and attain the Way must have planted their roots of virtue in one or two or even five lifetimes. Actually, they have already evolved to a very high level. Thus, when they learn the truth contained in these teachings, their hearts may immediately reconnect with the integral nature of the multi-universe. Then the omniscient, omnipresent Integral One, which is the Treasure of Divine Power of the multi-universe, will shine upon them and absorb them into its radiance. They will become submerged in the boundless ocean of blessings and impersonal love of the Integral One.

"Why is this so? Those people will have dissolved their rigid mental concepts of self and others, male and female, longevity and brevity, life and death. Also, they will not have any mental obstructions formed by different cultural backgrounds, customs, or religious beliefs which would prevent the perception of the subtle truth of universal integration. To hold the mind within any rigid framework is to immediately become trapped in the bondage of duality. If one does not discriminate between what is labeled as sacred and profane, one is liberated from the bondage of all concepts. Thus one should not embrace any religious concept or mental structure that is formed while living in the physical world. All mental structures must finally be relinquished if one is to reach the ultimate and subtle truth of oneness."

⌐· 8 ·⌐

The master said, "Kind prince, what do you think? Has the Integral One invented something to teach us?"

"No, Venerable Teacher," replied the prince, "the Integral One has invented nothing to teach."

"Kind prince, what do you think? Have I attained an awareness which is beyond the integral truth? Have I established a personal teaching which is separate from the Universal Way?"

"Venerable Teacher, according to my understanding, there is nothing definite or set which can lead one to reach the integral truth. Nor is unconditioned awareness a set or rigid way of perceiving things. Why is this? All true guidance is intangible because the Universal Way is beyond the limits of the mind. The Universal Way is neither religious nor worldly. All of the far-reaching, unfaded teachings of the ancient sages come from the same source: the subtle truth of great oneness. Different expressions are merely the result of different times and places."

"What do you think, kind prince?" asked the master. "Suppose a person amasses a worldly treasure and then gives it all away to those in need. According to the universal law of energy response, will he derive blessings in proportion to the treasure he gives away?"

"Yes, Venerable Teacher, there will be abundant blessings derived from this."

"Kind prince, if someone cherishes the guidance of these teachings, and uses it to instruct others and serve them selflessly, the blessings of this person will be far greater than those of the former. Why is this?"

"Venerable Teacher, if one amasses wealth and gives it away in the hope of receiving blessings, he earns his blessings by striving and therefore remains in the realm of duality. The one who practices the Universal Way and then guides others gives spontaneously whatever he has, simply because it is his nature to do so; thus he derives his blessings through nonaction and never deviates from the Universal Way."

"Kind prince, true blessings and impersonal love are beyond the concept of measurement. When we start to be concerned about blessings, they cease to be blessings."

ᴗ· 10 ·ᴖ

"Kind prince," said the master, "suppose a person cuts himself loose from being fooled by the senses. Can he then become attached to the fruit of his enlightenment?"

"No, my Venerable Teacher. The one who has succeeded in cutting himself loose from attachment to the senses cannot then fasten himself to what he has attained. To do so would be to return to the enslavement of the senses, and the reign of the ego would ruin what he had attained. Therefore, one cannot hold any idea in the mind about what one has attained."

"What do you think, kind prince? Suppose a person discovers that his life has been a ceaseless pattern of coming and going. Suppose further that he decides to make this journey his last and sets out to accomplish the final purification in order to live forever in the Realm of Integral Life. Can he become attached to the idea of the culmination of his final journey?"

"No, he cannot, Venerable Teacher. The one who discovers that life is a phenomenon of coming and going also discovers that there is no such thing as coming and going at the root of integral life. How, then, could he become attached to what is called the last journey of life?"

"Then, kind prince, what do you think? Can one who has achieved the state of desirelessness hold the notion of being happy to have finally reached the state of desirelessness? Or can one who has transcended life and death to enjoy the Universal Way be happy about his attainment?"

"No, Venerable Teacher. One who has already attained the final transcendence would not think about having transcended life and death. By creating the concepts of life and death, he would only trap himself again in the bondage of duality with its mental framework of self and others, longevity and brevity, life and death.

"Venerable Teacher, you have attested that I have purified myself so thoroughly that no desire or conflict remain and that I have attained the highest possible level of virtue. Yet I never think about having no desires. Because I do not hold anything particular in my mind, I am on the Universal Way. To be completely desireless is to achieve the true happiness of egolessness; it is the way of transcendental bliss."

⌐ 11 ⌐

The master said, "Kind prince, what do you think? When I was a disciple at my master's side, did I learn anything from my master that would make me feel sanctimonious?"

"No, Venerable Teacher, you learned nothing that would make you feel sanctimonious."

"Well then, kind prince, what do you think? Is the residence of the Integral One very sublime?"

"No, Venerable Teacher, where the Integral One resides cannot be defined in that manner. If it could be defined in that manner, it would not be the achievement of total integration which cannot be touched by a fragmented mind. Yet it may be called the Life of the Most Sublime. Therefore, one should keep one's mind pure, simple, plain, and untouched. One should not disintegrate one's mind by creating the dualistic concepts of different forms, sounds, smells, flavors, feelings, or anything else that fosters the illusion of separation. In order to reach complete integration, one must dedicate one's being wholly to the integral truth."

"Tell me, kind prince," said the master, "If someone's body were as big as the Mountain of Enormity, do you think his body would be very large?"

"It would be huge, Venerable Teacher. But why do you ask such a question?"

"Kind prince, the formless body of integral truth is immeasurably huge!"

~· 12 ·~

The master continued his instruction. "Kind prince, if there were as many rivers in the world as there are grains of sand in the River of Timelessness, and if each river contained as much sand as the River of Timelessness, do you think that would be a vast amount of sand?"

"Yes, indeed, Venerable Teacher, it would be very vast."

"Kind prince, if a person amassed a huge fortune and gave it all away to help as many people as there are grains of sand in the River of Timelessness, would the blessing that he gained be as great as what he gave?"

"It would be very great indeed, Venerable Teacher, because returning an equivalent response is the nature of the subtle law of the universe."

"That is true, kind prince, but if one practiced the truth contained in these teachings and expounded it to others, the benevolent grace and blessings he would evoke from the universe would be even greater. When someone elucidates this sacred scripture to others, the place in which he does so becomes sacred and is respected by all spiritual beings, those with form as well as those without. Wherever these teachings are, the Sacred Altar is. All the virtuous beings of the universe pay homage to it, and the divine guardians of the eight powerful energy rays protect it. All people should reverently offer salutations and incense to it and surround it with fragrant flowers.

"Furthermore, if someone embraces the integral truth contained in this scripture, and studies and practices it, then he must attain the highest blessing of all beings. All of the great masters of the Universal Way respond to those who cherish it."

∽· 13 ·∽

"Kind prince," asked the master, "what do you think? Are all the small particles that make up the universe numerous?"

"Yes, very numerous, Venerable Teacher."

"And, kind prince, do you think the universe is very vast?"

"It is vast indeed, Venerable Teacher."

"But, kind prince, to the Integral One, the particles are not small nor is the universe vast. It is merely the relative mind that labels them so.

"Kind prince, what do you think? Can one imagine the Integral One as having any kind of wonderful form?"

"No, Venerable Teacher, one cannot imagine the Integral One as having any kind of wonderful form, because to the Integral One form is not real; it is merely labeled as such."

"Now, kind prince, if there are good men and women who offer their lives in service to others, their blessings will certainly be bountiful. But if someone practices the truth contained in the lines and chapters of this scripture, and expounds it to others, his blessings will be immeasurably abundant."

⌁ 14 ⌁

At that time the prince wholly understood the wonderful teaching that the master had given him. He could not help bursting into tears with deep sadness for his past ignorance, and he said, "Venerable Teacher, this is the most profound instruction I have heard since I first began developing my own insight. It is truly the highest teaching. I am deeply grateful to you for your instruction and I vow to practice this truth joyfully as the sacred fulfillment of my life.

"I wonder, though, if many generations from now,

there will be people who will discover this instruction and be able to practice it joyfully in their daily lives. If so, these individuals would be most unusual, for they would have dissolved all mental concepts of ego, self and others, male and female, longevity and brevity, and life and death. Those who dissolve all concepts of individuality are beings of absolute awareness. By regaining Oneness with the clarity of their minds, they would fulfill the most virtuous merit and attain the highest blessing."

"Very true, kind prince. If someone in the future embraces this revelation of the integral life without skepticism, conflict, or panic, then this person would be very, very unusual.

"Kind prince, if we label integral Oneness as subtle and transcendental, then it ceases to be true integral Oneness. By doing this, we reduce it to the mental sphere of dichotomy where it is no longer the essential, direct, and undistorted reflection of universal truth of one life."

⁓ 15 ⁓

The master continued, "Kind prince, tolerance is a necessary virtue in everyone's daily life, but for an integral being there is nothing that needs to be tolerated or labeled as tolerance. Tolerance exists only in the relative sphere.

"Why is this? If someone does something unpleasant to us, we need to gather our strength to bear it; it is a difficult and disagreeable situation. However, if you have risen above the relative concepts of the mind, there is no self or others, no longevity or brevity, no life or death in your mind, so there is no hatred or resentment. What, then, is the necessity for tolerance?

"Kind prince, a person who is highly evolved leaves behind all concepts of individuality and extends impersonal love to include all existence. Dissolving individuality enables one to free oneself from the entangling discriminations of form, language, sense perception, feeling, and all other relative conditions. It allows one's true being to grow freely without the hindrance of attachment. When the mind is attached to something, it can hold little more than self-created pain. One who is highly evolved, therefore, is attached to nothing and does not depend on any particular mental concept or form in his relations with people or in serving them. His very being benefits all life.

"To an integral being, all form is equal to that which is formless. All life is equal to all nonlife. Kind prince, this is the reality of the universe; it is the subtle, integral truth and not a religious invention. There is no need for further commentary, for the instruction of transcendental, central reality is beyond the realm of trueness and falseness in ordinary logic. Only the individual who has already evolved to a high level may receive this precious instruction."

~ 16 ~

"Kind prince, suppose there are good men and women who offer as much of themselves as there is sand in the River of Timelessness to help people in the morning, and as much of themselves as there is sand in the River of Timelessness to help people in the afternoon, and then as much of themselves as there is sand in the River of Timelessness to help people in the evening. Suppose, too, that they continue to do this for eon after eon for the purpose of receiving virtuous blessings.

"Now suppose there are people who hear this sacred scripture and joyfully break through all obstacles in order to follow it. The blessings of these people will be even greater yet, for this scripture has boundless power.

"The Integral One reveals the truth contained in this scripture to those who cultivate themselves, not for their own sake, nor only half for their sake and half for others. The Integral One reveals this profundity to those who cultivate themselves for the sake of all, for this is the highest level of virtue. If there is someone who accepts this truth and who studies, practices, and teaches it widely, then this person will certainly be acknowledged by the integral beings of the divine realm. This person will truly accomplish the great merit of shouldering the responsibility of transmitting the divine revelation.

"Kind prince, many people are pleased and satisfied with the various limited religious doctrines existing in the world today. They all hope to live in the Kingdom of

Heaven someday and sit sublimely at the side of their personal deity, but by entertaining such hopes and beliefs they only foster concepts of self and others, longevity and brevity, life and death, and so on without end. With such conceptual entanglements they cannot even listen to the truth, much less study, practice, and embrace it or explain it to others. In this case, how can they ever uplift themselves to the subtle, central realm to be with the Integral One of One Universal Life?"

⌒ 17 ⌒

The master continued, "Kind prince, if good men and women study and embrace this scripture, yet are scorned by others, this is the result of the ignorant actions of their past lives that are bearing bad fruit in this life. Through continuing to study and practice the truth contained in this scripture, however, their energy will be cleansed and they will attain the crystal clear awareness of an integral being.

"Kind prince, after I received my birth from the Subtle Origin, I dedicated myself through many lifetimes to innumerable religions and their deities, believing that they would act as intermediaries between me and the subtle, integral reality of the universe. I did not neglect or overlook a single one of them. Yet, if someone in the distant future, in the Age of Confusion for instance, were to directly embrace the integral truth contained in this scripture, the virtue he would embody and the merit he would attain would be much, much greater than what I attained through my long religious dedication. This is because he would be aware of his own divine nature through direct contact with it, not through the indirect process of worshiping others who have achieved the integral truth.

"Those who turn to deities as intermediaries between themselves and the subtle truth are like beggars who look outside themselves for the very treasure contained within their own nature. It is only after one discovers one's own divine nature that prayer or any form of worshiping the one universal life can be a true and effective spiritual cultivation of the wholeness of eternal life.

"Kind prince, as I just mentioned, if there are good people in the future who can embrace the truth contained in this scripture and who can study and practice it with great sincerity, the merit and virtue they will attain shall be immeasurable. You see, kind prince, this scripture is the subtle truth of one integral universal life, and the responsive power of the Universal Way neglects no one and can be denied by no one!"

～ 18 ～

At that time, the prince asked the master again, "Venerable Teacher, if good men and women are motivated to attain correct awareness in order to restore their integral nature, how can they maintain this awareness and subdue the delusive activity of the mind?"

The master replied, "Kind prince, good people who are motivated to attain the correct awareness of an integral being should dissolve all conceptions of duality. With integral awareness of their moral responsibility, they will be able to help all people to eliminate the darkness of the dichotomous mind and the delusions stemming from concepts of existence and nonexistence so that they can finally attain the essence of integral subtle transcendence. When this has been achieved, the one who renders service to others discovers that, in truth, there is no one being served; he no longer perceives other lives as external to himself, nor does he perceive his own existence as separate and individual. If integral beings still held any concepts of self and others, longevity and brevity, life and death, then they would not be beings of true integral awareness.

"Kind prince, what do you think? Did I attain awareness of the integral nature of the universe through the use of any special esoteric method?"

"No, Venerable Teacher," replied the prince, "As I understand, what you teach us is not something that can be obtained through the practice of any esoteric method, for there is no specific device that can uplift one to the higher realms. Once something is labeled as the ultimate method or device, it has already become a hindrance to one's attainment of integral awareness. Therefore, to an integral being, any external, established means is not the Universal Way."

"You are right, kind prince. There truly is no way for

an Integral One to separate his being from the nature of the universe. If I had used any particular way to attain awareness of the integral nature of the universe, then the masters who live in the deep central realm of one great life would not have recognized me as an integral being. They refer to me, however, as a cosmic person who lives in all times and places, and this is what an integral being should be.

"If there is someone who states that an Integral One has attained the correct awareness of the integral nature of the universe by means of any specific way, then he is simply mistaken. There is no relative, specific way in which one can achieve awareness of the integral truth. The integral nature of the universe cannot be distinguished through a dualistic mode of perception. Therefore, an Integral One teaches only the Universal Way of life. What are labeled as methods of achieving enlightenment and uplifting one to the higher realms, wise prince, do not exist in the integral realm.

"Kind prince, one of integral virtue is selfless and impartial. When my fellow students and I studied with our teacher, no one received special attention or instruction for his own particular benefit. The teacher gave the same instruction to all of us and it was up to each student to absorb, digest, and develop the teaching within himself. A student should not attempt to provoke special attention or instruction from his teacher, nor should he attempt to sway the teacher to show a personal preference for him. Some people try very hard to impress a deity in whom they believe in order to invoke special favors or blessings, but this is only a fantasy that demonstrates the person's lack of true spiritual development. Unconditional sincerity is what evokes a response from the subtle realm of universal divine power.

"For a teacher to impart his wisdom to others is purely a realization of his virtue. A student should not try to disturb his teacher with emotional or material entanglements of any kind, because the gross energy of mental, physical, or emotional entanglement severs the subtle spiritual connection with the divine energy. If a disciple is excessively emotional or if his mind is very rigid, good teachings will be distorted and the teacher's wisdom will not be assimilated. If the teacher must continually work on the student's mental problems, he is prevented from sharing his spiritual treasure with the student. The student should not insist that the teacher solve his problems or do the inner work that is an essential aspect of one's own cultivation. Instead, the student should eliminate all obstacles and make himself an empty vessel to receive the light of One Great Life from his teacher."

⌐· 19 ·¬

"Kind prince," asked the master, "how do we recognize the size of the body which humankind possesses?"

The prince replied, "Venerable Teacher, according to the Universal Way, the vast body possessed by humankind is not vast, but is merely called so. It is not bigger or smaller than any other kind of life."

"Kind prince, this understanding is the foundation of correct awareness. If a person says that he should help all people by sharing his correct awareness with them, he shows that he does not truly have correct awareness. Why is this? An integral being has no perception of self and others, life and death, longevity and brevity. If there is no self, there are no others to help through sharing one's awareness.

"Kind prince, if one of correct awareness states that the temple is holy and sublime, he does not truly have correct awareness because an integral being labels nothing. People may label a temple as holy and sublime by creating the dualistic concept of places which are holy and sublime in contrast to places which are not. Only when one has dissolved all discrimination, however, can he be recognized as having attained correct awareness of integralness. Kind prince, ignore all appearances of duality and embrace only the integral, one universal life."

⁓· 20 ·⁓

"Kind prince, what do you think?" asked the master. Does the Integral One have physical eyes?"

"Yes, Venerable Teacher, the Integral One has physical eyes."

"What do you think, kind prince? Does the Integral One have spiritual eyes?"

"Indeed, Venerable Teacher, the Integral One has spiritual eyes which can see through all things."

"Kind prince, what do you think? Has the Integral One special eyes of wisdom?"

"Yes, Venerable Teacher, the Integral One has eyes of wisdom."

"Kind prince, what do you think? Does the Integral One have unusual eyes which discern all kinds of spiritual paths?"

"Yes, Venerable Teacher, the Integral One has outstanding eyes which can perceive all things and all spiritual paths."

"Kind prince, does the Integral One have integral eyes?"

"Yes, Venerable Teacher, the Integral One has integral eyes that are incomparable to all other eyes."

"Kind prince, people with clairvoyance may see things that are not within sight, but they cannot see the formless. People with clairaudience may hear special sounds, but they cannot hear the soundless. People with telepathy may communicate directly with another being's mind, but they cannot communicate with people who have achieved no-mind. People with telekinetic ability may move things without physically touching them, but they cannot move the intangible.

"Kind prince, all of these abilities exist only in the realm of duality. They lose their meaning before the Integral One, for to the Integral One there is nothing which can be called clairvoyance, clairaudience, telepathy, or telekinesis. These are things that are merely labeled so."

"Kind prince, what do you think? Does the Integral One refer to the sand in the River of Timelessness as sand?"

"Yes, Venerable Teacher, the Integral One refers to the sand in the River of Timelessness as sand."

"Kind prince, what do you think? If there were as many rivers as there are grains of sand in the River of Timelessness, and if there were as many worlds as there are grains of sand in all the rivers, would that be very many?"

"Very many, indeed, Venerable Teacher."

"Kind prince, the sand is truly no different from the world, and the world is no different from the sand. People form their minds in countless ways and the Integral One knows all of them. How? To the Integral One the mind is not real. The mind of the past cannot be kept, the mind of the present cannot be held, and the mind of the future cannot be caught. Yet people are attached to such delusions and label them as mind.

"Kind prince, it is not the mind which varies constantly, but events which are ever changing. The events of the past cannot be kept, the events of the present cannot be held, and the events of the future cannot be caught. But the mind is too easily possessed by such images. If events themselves do not seize the mind and totally absorb one's consciousness, then the preconceptions and preoccupations of the mind prevent one from true awareness of the event. When these deviations occur, trouble is sure to follow. An enjoyable past event cannot be held, and the bright future is delayed by one's anxiety. Beautiful present circumstances cannot be preserved. All good things seem fragile and fleeting. Dissolve attachment to these things and embrace only integral oneness. Integral awareness is not far in the distance; clarity is close at hand."

~· 22 ·~

The master said, "Kind prince, what do you think? Can the Integral One be seen as having a beautiful physical appearance?"

"No, Venerable Teacher, the Integral One cannot be seen as having a beautiful physical appearance, because to the Integral One the possession of a beautiful form is equal to the possession of no-form. It is only relatively named so."

"What do you think, then, kind prince? Does the Integral One present all kinds of wonders and perform miracles in order to show off his divine majesty or inspire faith and obedience in others?"

"No, Venerable Teacher, the Integral One does not present itself in that way, because to present wonders and perform miracles for such purposes is not its nature."

"Kind prince, the subtle body of the Integral One is omnipresent. It always exists, and it presents itself when all speech has been exhausted and the mind has been stripped away. When crystal clarity and unadulterated purity appear, the subtle body of the Integral One appears. When the highest sincerity is achieved, the subtle cosmic body of the Integral One responds. Then, wise prince, the Integral One can be seen even in what appears to be plain, simple, and ordinary."

⌐· 23 ·⌐

"Kind prince, please do not suppose that an integral being imposes any particular doctrine on people. If someone says that an integral being sets up a particular religious teaching to transmit the truth, he is ignorant of the Universal Way and does not truly understand what I have said. The most achieved of teachers actually has nothing to say. Although what he teaches may be called the highest truth, the reality can never be put into words."

At that time the prince asked the master, "Venerable Teacher, when people hear this truth in the future, will they be able to follow it?"

"Kind prince, do not worry about whether there will be people to follow it or not. An integral being knows that nothing which can be put into words is the integral truth. He does not ask people to follow, his only interest is to serve. He does not indulge in worry, but simply does his work. This is called 'doing that which is done by not-doing.'"

~· 24 ·~

The prince addressed the master once again. "Venerable Teacher, according to the Universal Way, when one attains subtle universal awareness he should not label it an achievement. Is that correct?"

The master kindly answered, "Yes, this is very true, dear prince. I have received nothing from the attainment of unconditional awareness. Awareness of the integral nature of the universe is indescribable; it cannot be contained by any word or name. If a person thinks in terms of attaining something, that means he believes there is something to obtain or achieve external to his own nature. It means that he fails to realize that his own true nature is the integral nature of the universe itself."

~· 25 ·~

The master continued, "Moreover, kind prince, the Integral One reveals itself in the equality of the nature of all things. In reality, nothing is high or low. To be aware of this is to know the Universal Way.

"When one has no awareness of self and others or of life and death, and when one lives one's life with sincerity, then every moment and every activity are an expression of the bondage-free truth. It is no longer necessary to attain a transcendental awareness of the integral nature of the universe.

"Kind prince, all spiritual paths are not true paths that can lead one to the Integral Realm of universal oneness. People may call them spiritual, but in reality they are only mental constructs. Follow only the Universal Way, embrace only Oneness, and ignore all divergence."

∽· 26 ·∾

The prince was very much enlightened at this time and with great humility he said, "Venerable Teacher, your precious guidance has illuminated the two kinds of blessings: worldly blessings, which are planted by good deeds and almsgiving, and which are limited in time and space by the conditioned mind, and integral blessing, which is derived from the expression of integral awareness in all aspects of life. This awareness frees one from the bondage of the conditioned body, mind, and spirit. Once freed, one can emerge into the integral realm to live here and now. This blessing is boundless and unquestionable.

"Venerable Teacher, you have also illuminated the two kinds of wisdom. Worldly wisdom can help one understand worldly things, but it is only conceptual understanding and thus hinders the direct experience of the truth. Understanding always comes one moment after the experience itself and therefore cannot be direct enlightenment which dissolves both subject and object. While integral wisdom sometimes appears to be the opposite of worldly wisdom, it too can help connect one to worldly things, but in this case the connection of the mind with reality is not through any pattern of understanding but through direct participation in the experience of life. The observer and the object of observation are dissolved without hindrance of preconception or delayed understanding. It is not necessary to accumulate mental attitudes after an experience has taken place, because to be is to know. This is the way of integral being.

"Integral blessing and wisdom transcend all relative blessings and wisdom. If someone amasses a vast amount of wealth and gives it away to the needy, the blessing he can receive through this is tremendous, but such a blessing is only one billionth of a billionth of the amount of blessing that is bestowed on one who practices and guides others to the Universal Way expounded in this scripture."

⁓· 27 ·⁓

"Kind prince," said the master, "please do not think that an integral being holds the idea of conveying people to the integral realm. Why? Because there are no people to be conveyed to the integral realm.

"There is no 'self,' yet worldly people believe that a self exists. Wise prince, to an integral being so-called worldly people are not worldly, they are only titled so. Worldlings and immortals, the unaware and the enlightened, all originally have the same nature as the Subtle Path itself. There is not the slightest difference in their true nature."

"Kind prince," continued the master, "what do you think? Can one observe the appearance of the Integral One in all kinds of beautiful forms?"

"It could be so, Venerable Teacher. The appearance of the Integral One could be seen as the model of universal perfection."

"Kind prince, if one discerns the Integral One in all kinds of beautiful forms, then all the luminous heavenly bodies in the sky would be the subtle cosmic body of the Integral One."

The prince then told the master, "Venerable Teacher, according to my present understanding of the Integral Way, one should not mistake the subtle cosmic body of the Integral One as having form in the relative sense."

At that time, the master affirmed the prince's answer by saying:

> If one sees the Integral One in a particular form,
> If one searches for the Integral One in a particular tone,
> Such a person practices sorcery and can never see the subtle cosmic body of the Integral One.

"Kind prince," said the master, "if you think that an integral being attains total awareness without relying on relative practices and with no need of proper discipline or necessary rituals, then you have the wrong idea. My most important request is that you do not think that by giving up these postures, rituals, manners, disciplines, and practices one can attain infinite awareness of the omnipresent truth. These things can help channel one's emotions as well as the total life energy itself. It can be an effective process of refinement for molding a beginner into the correct shape for life.

"Kind prince, do not misunderstand and think that one who has attained the highest, unconditional awareness should reject the natural, fundamental truth, common sense, definable practices, moral law, and virtuous conduct; this way of thinking will not lead to complete awareness but only to monomania. One who is motivated to attain the highest integral awareness does not reject the practice of a simple, virtuous life, a healthy regimen, and integral-mindedness. Without good self-discipline, one falls apart again, loses the awareness he has attained, and returns to the darkness he left behind. Though the road to achievement is always open to one who has been there, one cannot be sure of never falling back again. There are many spiritual practitioners, therefore, who are in a constant flux of up and down, never respecting the consistency of good self-discipline.

"Wise prince, to practice all these essential disciplines is to live the Universal Way of Life and the ultimate truth of nature, beyond all relative principles and fragmentary ideas. All the unnecessary beliefs and activities of worldly life impair the well-being of an individual and spoil the peace and harmony of human relations.

"Kind prince, one who follows the Universal Way helps those who are spiritually undeveloped and who rely on transitory, illusory images and methods before reaching the ultimate truth. One who follows the Universal Way does not deny the importance of making the correct effort to achieve a positive, plain, healthy, and natural life. This is because one who follows the Universal Way does not hold the erroneous view that life is merely an individualized, physical phenomenon and that all consciousness ceases at death.

"Wise prince, if one who practices virtue amasses worldly treasures as numerous as the grains of sand in the River of Timelessness and gives them as alms to the needy but another practices virtue in all aspects of life, selflessly and with incomparable perseverance, the fulfillment of the latter is so great it is unfathomable.

"Kind prince, virtuous beings never take advantage of others nor do they desire favor or reward for their virtuous actions."

Then the prince asked the master, "Venerable Teacher, why is it that those who are virtuous do not have the virtue to accept blessings that are the result of their actions?"

"Kind prince, virtuous beings practice virtue without any personal consideration. When I say that they do not accept the rewards of their virtuous behavior, I mean that they do nothing to spoil the unconditional quality of their virtue. Thus, they are integral beings. In order to achieve the Universal Way of life, it is essential that one take no thought of the personal benefit that results from one's virtuous behavior. This is the way to fulfill one's own integral nature.

"Kind prince, one who is integrally virtuous does not sit back and enjoy the loftiness of his personal spiritual achievement while the world engages in bloodshed because of people's ignorant attachments to particular ideologies and theologies. One of integral virtue is not interested in personal exaltation. He exposes the truth and shows the way for the evolution of all humanity. Any individual's spiritual achievement can never be considered great as long as the world is victimized by wars.

"Kind prince, those who brandish power are like small children playing with an enormous ax; they will inevitably bring about their own destruction. Undeveloped humanity can destroy itself through its own ignorance, and this is why one of integral virtue has something of great value to say and share with people. His purpose is not to share the excellence of his mind nor to display his great compassion. It is simply the natural responsibility of one who can see to tell a blind horseman on a blind horse that he is riding toward an abyss."

The prince asked, "Venerable Teacher, I have only a minor question. I think I understand, but I am not sure. You often speak of integral awareness as the awareness of wholeness, complete awareness, and bondage-free awareness. Would you please explain this further to my limited mind?"

"Kind prince," replied the master, "awareness is the

subtle movement of the mind. It is different than thought in that it can be reflective and light up your own mistakes as well as those of others. In general, awareness is conditioned by momentary reflections of things or symbols. It is something that can send your mind deep into further levels of understanding; thus, your question is not a minor one but a great one. The integral truth of one universal life is achieved by the attainment of integral awareness and whole enlightenment. These are key spiritual offerings to all who are willing to reach for them. They are one in matter of fact, although I have spoken of them as separate things so that my listeners can understand. One of integral awareness and whole enlightenment sees the physical world of the sun, moon, and stars, which extends to the Silver River (the galaxy) and the Star Clouds (nebulae), as different parts of one's physical body. Highly evolved souls become the soul of the physical multi-universe. Depending on the development of the individual's mind and spirit, one can discover not only the great universal body but achieve true awareness and enlightenment of the soul and the reality of one universal life."

∽ 30 ∽

"Venerable Teacher, it is clear that if one person offers worldly treasures as alms to those in need while another person practices the Integral Way of life and expounds its truth to others, the blessings of the latter will be much greater than those of the former, for one who expounds the Integral Way is able to avoid the extreme of partialism."

The master replied by saying, "Kind prince, this kind of relative comparison may have some value, but the highest teaching is wordless because the subtle integral truth itself is unspeakable, unexplainable, and unthinkable. One who tries to talk about it only deviates from it and makes it obscure. One who thinks about it loses it. All we can do, therefore, is show the way to the traveler; we cannot walk it for him. We can write the prescription, but we cannot drink the bitter herbal tea for him. All teachings are like medicine which is given to the sick according to the disease they have.

"There is no single word which can be held as the total truth, there is only the Universal Way of life. An integral being lives quietly, connecting himself with the wordless truth of life undividedly, selflessly, and harmoniously."

"In this case, Venerable Teacher, is it correct to say that, according to the integral truth, those who offer alms to people in need and those who expound the Universal Way accumulate blessings equal to nothing?"

"Kind prince," replied the master, "the blessings are neither something nor nothing. Both the offering of alms and the expounding of the Universal Way are manifestations of positive energy which will evoke a corresponding response from the universe.

"Kind prince, what do you think? Can beauty be put into words?"

"No, Venerable Teacher, true beauty speaks for itself."

"Tell me, kind prince, can perfection be put into words?"

"No, Venerable Teacher, true perfection speaks for itself."

"Kind prince, can the integral truth be put into words?"

"No, Venerable Teacher, it, too, speaks for itself."

"Kind prince, there are two kinds of disciples who follow the Universal Way. One kind understands it intellectually and is able to speak about it well while the other actually lives it with his whole being."

⁓· 31 ·⁓

The master continued, "Kind prince, if someone thinks that the subtle cosmic body of the Integral One comes and goes, sits and lies down, then this individual has not understood what I am saying. Why? Because the subtle cosmic body comes and goes nowhere, yet is always everywhere. Although it is called the subtle cosmic body, its reality cannot be put into words. To be aware of being with the Integral One is like watching the reflection of the moon on the surface of a still lake. Actually, the moon is not in the lake, yet people speak of it so. If, by chance, clouds appear and cover the moon, people say that it has departed from the lake, yet it has actually gone nowhere. The relationship between the universal soul and the individual soul is just like the relationship between the moon and the lake. Spiritual security is always present, but the clouds of the mind create the phenomena of apparent separation. The true nature of the universe is always self-existent, never failing to respond to an individual's straight and direct awareness. If an individual is aware enough, he realizes that the Integral One does not come only at the time of awareness. When one's mind is disturbed or confused, the Integral One seems to disappear, yet one's true nature has not departed. One creates the darkness which covers the light that is always available to freely support one's soul.

"It is the double vision of the mind which leads people to create mischief, agony, misery, and tragedy. The source of all suffering is an individual's stubborn adherence to the establishment of self which separates him from his integral nature. It is not that the Universal Way chooses to be with one person and not another.

"There are no images which should be held on to and no blessings which should be sought. There is no single virtue on which one should focus, nor any special names one should revere. Thus, when one attains integral awareness he can directly rejoin his true nature, which is the subtle cosmic body of the Integral One."

"Kind prince, if someone could smash the universe into small bits, do you think there would be very many particles?"

"There would be very many indeed, Venerable Teacher, but only if they really existed individually. To the Integral One, the individual small particles would not be individual small particles; they are merely named so. The same holds true for the numerous worlds in the universe; they are not numerous to the Integral One, but are merely named so. The so-called worlds are but the conjoining of the individual small particles. To the Integral One, the occurrence of conjoining is not real but is merely called so."

"Kind prince, each small particle is an entire world in itself. The worlds are the conjoint movement of small particles. There is no real difference between small particles and the vast world, but they are differently named because of the relative concepts of small and vast. When the small particles gather, there is the world; when the world disperses, there are small particles. It is not accurate to say they are different. Neither is it accurate to say that the world is a heap of small particles with varied formations, nor that the small particles conjoin and gather as the world. One cannot be distinguished as being primary and the other as secondary because in reality there is no difference between the two.

"There are no grounds for believing that the movement of conjoining and dispersing is either with or without purpose. Nor are there any grounds for commenting on whether those movements are the mischief of blind, mechanical, physical nature or the wonderful creation of an artistic, universal mind. It is all the same when one has the insight to see the deep nature of things. It is different when one is bewildered by the diversified movements on the surface of reality. When people hold fast to their egos, they are bewildered by the question of whether it is the same thing or different, thus it is the ego which blinds people to the great equality of integral reality. The relative concepts of sameness and difference are merely manipulations of the mind and have nothing to do with reality. They preoccupy one with mere names and prevent the direct perception of reality.

"The world and the particles are not separate, isolated things. The particles could be gathered to become the world, and the world could be dispersed to become particles. One small particle contains the nature of the world, and the world contains the nature of each small particle; the nature of each is the same. Thus, although they are not one and the same, neither are they different. If one is attached to names, however, one can never achieve a clear, direct perception of the integral truth of all things.

"Kind prince, each small particle is a world of matter. At the same time, it is a world of spirituality. It possesses both spirituality and materiality. Likewise, every event is a conjoint entity of many different elements. In reality, each conjoint entity is not an isolated, single event, but is only regarded and named as such. The apparently single event is a variation and segment of the great whole. The great whole is the combination of all single events. The single events contain the life experience of the whole. The great whole contains the life substance of the single events and vice versa. Thus, in reality, there is no discrimination between single events and the great whole; both are equal.

"Everything in the universe is equal. The great equality of reality comprises the subtle cosmic body of the Integral One. However, the direct perception of this Oneness is blocked by established mental concepts which separate us from the truth of integral being.

"Kind prince, ignore both the world and the particles, the single event and the conjoint mass. Embrace only the unnamable Oneness."

ᴗ·33·ᴖ

The master continued, "Wise prince, the individual body is the cosmic body. This refers not only to humankind, but to all beings. The cosmic body is not separate from the individual body, nor is the individual body separate from the cosmic body.

"The small particle which I referred to before is associated with the individual body. When the world diversifies into small particles, it is like the cosmic body appearing as the individual body. Just as the small particles gather, comprising the vast world, the individual actualizes the cosmic body. The cosmic body must not be thought of as something separate from the whole, for it is whole itself and generates all individual bodies. Though the small particles individually may not be the world, together they may comprise the body of the world. While the world may not be the small particles, it could be traced back to the small particles.

"The cosmic body may be comprehended as the vast and profound universe, but it is not observable in physical terms. It is beyond reach, yet at the same time it is also within reach.

"The relationship between the world and the small particles is somewhat similar to the relationship between a flower and a mirror which reflects it. The mirror reflects the flower, and through this reflection the existence of the mirror may be perceived. But in the relationship between the small particles and the world, it cannot be decided which side is the reflection and which is being reflected. Both reflect each other; neither can be held as the substance.

"The relationship between the cosmic body and the individual body is something like the relationship between the moon and its reflection on a lake. One side seems to be the real thing and the other just its reflection, but even the moon is only reflecting the light of the sun, and the sun is not the final source either. There is nothing substantial which is final.

"When small particles take on some configuration,

they may appear solid and fixed; however, they are neither solidly formed nor perpetually changing. It seems true that the world really exists in time and space, but it is merely a transient, conjoint event in this place and time. It also seems true that the individual body really exists in time and space, but it too is merely a transient, conjoint event in this place and time. Even the structure of time and space themselves is not real, but is only a conceptual creation. In the totality of truth, all things are not one and the same, but neither are they different. Their configuration as a conjoint entity does not last forever, but neither are they isolated and separate forever. To the Integral One, conjoint movement is only an illusion, as is dispersion, yet the mind labels them as being distinct. Integral reality is always beyond any attempt of the mind to categorize or make distinctions about it."

∽· 34 ·∼

"Very well, kind prince," said the master, "What do you think? Can small particles gather together to become a soul?"

"Venerable Teacher, when a star exists, its light exists. When the star disappears, its light also disappears; the star's subtle energy, however, does not die away. It either remains in the subtle realm or transfers to those connected with it.

"Human life and all things in the universe begin in the subtle realm of the unmanifest and are then brought forth into the realm of the manifest where they assume physical form. A human being is certainly a gathering of small particles and, when one is alive, the vitality is there. When one passes away the vitality disperses, but not the subtle energy. The energy may remain in the subtle realm or be transferred to those who may connect with it according to the law of energy response.

"What I wish to know, Venerable Teacher, is how long the life force of a human being can last."

"Kind prince, the potency of a human being can last very long indeed. In one lifetime a person may be born into a family or race or society or nation that he once loved, while in another lifetime he will be born into a family or race or society or nation toward which he was hostile. The person may be born with a shape that was once attractive to him or with one which disgusted him. Emotional attachment such as love or hate is heavy, gross energy, and it is this kind of energy that influences how one forms one's new life and environment in response to what one has projected mentally, emotionally, and physically."

∼· 35 ·∼

"Venerable Teacher," asked the prince, "when a person passes away, does his cognition pass with him in his future lives?"

"Kind prince, the basic function and ability of cognition continues its growth when a soul is reborn into the physical world, however, the content of cognition is generally not carried with the soul. This is especially true of those people who have spent many years in intellectual pursuits. Except for the deep experience of certain training that is strongly built and forged, knowledge is stripped away because the storage of such information is related to the brain cells rather than to basic patterns and deep instincts of life."

"Venerable Teacher, can intuitional ability be passed on from one lifetime to the next?"

"Kind prince, insight is not the content of knowledge. Because it is not of the realm of the intellect, it continues whenever and wherever the being exists."

"Venerable Teacher, can it be said that insight is immortal, then?"

"Kind prince, it is the being which is immortal, and some of the ability. If a being develops his insight but does not achieve immortality, the insight will follow the same cycle of life, death, and rebirth that the person follows. If the person achieves immortality, however, he will be an immortal being with pure insight."

⌁ 36 ⌁

"Venerable Teacher, is it possible for an individual to uplift himself to the immortal realm and enjoy pure freedom and absolute happiness?"

"Kind prince," replied the master, "it is possible. Undiscriminating virtue is the vehicle that transports one there; it expresses the highest energy of universal nature. It brings forth all lives and offers support to the development of all human beings. It is the conjoint energy of high spiritual beings who respond to all energy of the same subtle frequency as their own. The most powerful protection one can have from negative influences is the whole virtue of a natural life. This is the simple reality of the law of energy response. Kind and selfless beings lead a life attuned to the Universal Way. With whole virtue they eliminate the artificial boundaries between societies and the illusory boundary between life and death. In this way they become immortal."

"Venerable Teacher, do all immortal divine beings have insight?"

"Kind prince, it is not a question of whether they have insight into one particular thing or not, but whether a being has cultivated and developed the vision of wholeness before realizing an integral life of immortality. If a person learns only the technique of gathering energy in order to become immortal, but does not develop his entire being and complete vision, then his cultivation depends entirely on the information he is able to gather. Even if he is fortunate enough to learn the right way from a secret book or special instruction, he will probe in darkness and may succeed in becoming immortal only by grace. Most likely, he will meet with many kinds of trouble before he ever gets that far, unless his virtue is complete."

"Venerable Teacher, if one develops insight through

practicing a secret system of self-cultivation, can he become an immortal without any difficulties?"

"Kind prince, it is not that those with knowledge of a secret system of self-cultivation do not encounter the problems of life, but rather that they are thoroughly equipped to deal with them successfully. One should not think of difficult situations as being trouble, but rather as the unfolding of a virtuous life and its subtle laws."

"Venerable Teacher, I understand that one who is cultivating himself in order to evolve to the immortal realm must not try to hide in a corner and avoid the reality of life. He must face the reality of worldly life, for the reality of one's cultivation and development lies in learning to solve all possible difficulties through the unfoldment of one's complete vision which sees the integral truth."

"Kind prince, there can be no complete development for those who do not live a complete life. A complete life is the foundation for the attainment of immortality. If an individual's energy is distorted and imbalanced because of partial development, this contradicts the law of existence and disintegrates the person's being. The result is not only the loss of possible immortality, but the very dissolution of life itself."

~ 37 ~

"Venerable Teacher, is an individual responsible for whether his life is pleasant or unpleasant and for whether it has a happy or unhappy ending? Is he also responsible for the lives of others?"

"Kind prince, after one takes form as an individual entity, suffering and enjoyment continue throughout many lifetimes and even during the subtle intermission between lives. Actually, to suffer and enjoy seems to be the destiny of an individual, but its extent is determined by the way in which one subjectively forms one's energy, consciously and unconsciously.

"With regard to whether a person is responsible for the lives of others, it is not a question of responsibility, but of how one manifests one's energy.

"Kind prince, what do you think? Is the subtle stage of life the root of one's life, and is the visible stage the tree? Or is the invisible stage the tree and the active stage the root?"

"Venerable Teacher, I now understand that each stage of life is the root of the next stage with each event as an element of the total event. This is the way one continuously forms one's life and destiny."

"Kind prince, to the Integral One there is no tree and no root. This means that there is no isolated, single event; all events are related. There is no tree, therefore, that is separate from its root, nor any root that is separate from the tree. Neither can it be separated from the soil, the climate, and the natural environment. The integrity of the tree depends on the normalcy of nature and the mercy of mankind. This also holds true for the life of a human being."

"Venerable Teacher, what is the relationship between a soul and its physical life?"

"Kind prince, take this pine tree as an example. It has strong roots, a stout trunk, numerous branches, twigs, cones, and needles, yet it started from a tiny seed. The original seed of that tree was formed from fire, wind, water, and earth; however, this combination alone does not make a tree. The most important components are the energy rays emanating from numerous remote stars and from the sun and the moon. The spontaneous integration of all these ingredients nurtures the chance of a new life and brings the beautiful tree to life.

"Kind prince, all plants, animals, races of people, and many kinds of insects are images and symbols of the energy of various natural environments and are associated with the network of rays from different stars. The first invisible 'seeds' of energy bestowed on the earth originated from this network of energy rays. In one ancient ceremonial ritual, the integrally developed ones stated the great truth of life by saying, 'Heaven is our father and Earth is our mother. All living things are our brothers and sisters.' We must respect and be at peace with all the various forms of life, no matter how different they may appear."

⌣· 38 ·⌣

"Venerable Teacher, I was told that the first being to appear in the world was called Pan Kou. In the beginning, the universe was like a round stone drum and, after many years, the density inside of the drum began to change. From this stone was born Pan Kou, who shaped the universe into Heaven and Earth and divided himself into many, many life beings. His name literally means 'big round drum.' Does this mean that the first human being and his descendants were shaped like drums or that all human beings are merely like someone living in a drum, not knowing what goes on outside the drum?"

"Kind prince, when I was at my teacher's side, I asked the very same question. My kind teacher sang a song to me in response. As well as I can recall it, I will sing it now to you.

The Song of Pan Kou

Old Pan Kou knows nothing about time
and nothing about space as well.
His life is self-natured and self-sufficient.
He needs to ask for nothing outside of his own being.
The genesis of the world is the exercise of his mind.
When his minds starts to think, the world starts to
    move.
The world has never been made by any special design.
Neither has an end ever been put to it.
Old Pan Kou swings his ax and chisels rhythmically,
and from it comes Heaven, but not as you think of it,

and Earth, but not as you see it.
Everything is the way it naturally is.
Since the young gods who are the descendants
of Pan Kou follow only impulse,
They make moves that disturb the world.
The wise and old ones sit still
and watch the chess games of the foolish.
All the changes in the world
are displayed upon the chess board.
Victory and defeat are decided by the
subtle elements behind the moves.
It can clearly be seen by the wise.
The wise who love their life and value
their words remain quiet and watch.
If the foolish gods only knew it,
there is perfect originalness before any move is made.
It is what offers beings the opportunity of life.
When an artificial move is made, the subtle root
    begins to die.
When peace is disturbed, the vital energy passes.
The kindness of old Pan Kou is expressed as
    harmonious nature.
The further downfall of his descendants
causes the knowledge of the treasures
that are hidden in nature to be lost.
They look everywhere for it, making wasteful,
    competitive moves.
If any of them knew to look at the example of old Pan
    Kou's life,
Could they live fully with the same divine,
immortal nature of old Pan Kou?

Old Pan Kou never made any unnatural moves.
The true path of divine life keeps moving with him.
If a person looks for the path outside himself,
he will find his shadow and depart from the true
  substance.
The diverging paths of life multiply greatly
with each generation.
The lost sheep cannot be found because of so many
  side paths.
Once the divergence is eliminated, all Heavens and
  Earths,
all lost sheep and old Pan Kou himself
return to original oneness.
The good and healthy world of endless life
starts generating again, without anyone's command.

"Kind prince, to have knowledge is to create doubt, and to have doubt is to create the need for knowledge. Let it suffice to say that the named was born from the unnamed. The describable world comes from the indescribable Source. Before the good life is spoiled, let everything be its own truth, for the truth of one individual is the truth of the entire universe. Let everything be united with the truth of its own being.

"The totality of truth presents itself to you every time you blink your eyes. It can dance on the tip of your eyelash. It stretches as far as the eye can see and fills as much as the mind can hold. It exists in every moment of time and every bit of space. Is there any instant which does not contain the truth of life? Is there any place which does not hold the truth of existence and nonexistence? Take the example of the pine tree. Which inch of the living tree is not the truth? Which hour that the tree lives is not the truth? Can anyone deny this?"

"Venerable Teacher, will people of future generations, during the Age of Confusion, be able to understand such truth?"

"Kind prince, in the future, in the Age of Confusion, people will create many obstacles to knowing the simple truth and hold fast to their own blindness and falsehoods. They will persuade others to follow them and will persecute unbelievers and even start wars against them.

"Kind prince, the one who searches for the truth loses it. The one who wishes to hold the truth causes it to slip away from him. Because one departs from his own nature to search for something external, he overlooks the truth of his own being. To be is to be true. The muchness and suchness of truth is included in this very second. If you miss the truth of this moment, a thousand galloping horses cannot catch up with it."

~· 39 ·~

"Venerable Teacher, is there a great creator of the universe, and did this creator bring forth all things and beings?"

"Kind prince, there is creation, but it itself is uncreated. There is transformation, but it itself is not transformed. The uncreated is able to create and re-create, and the untransformed is able to transform and retransform. That which is created cannot help producing of itself, and the transformed cannot help transforming of itself. By this is meant that there is no time and space without the production or transformation of things of themselves. This is the exhibition of yin and yang, metaphorically expressed as the swing of old Pan Kou's ax. The untransformed goes to and fro. The range of what goes to and fro is unlimitable. The Universal Way has neither beginnings nor end and is inexhaustible. As the Integral One says:

> The subtle essence of the universe is eternal.
> It is like an unfailing fountain of life which flows
>   forever in a vast and profound valley.
> It is called the Primal Female, the Mysterious Origin.
> The operation of the opening and closing
> of the Gate of the Origin performs
> the Mystical Intercourse of the universe.
> This Mystical Intercourse brings forth all things
> from the unseen sphere into the realm of the manifest.
> The Mystical Intercourse of yin and yang
> is the root of universal life.
> The subtle, gentle movement of the interplay
> between yin and yang never ceases.
> Its creativity and usefulness are boundless.

"Therefore, my kind prince, that which creates things is itself uncreated, and that which transforms things is itself nontransformed. Creation, transformation, form, appearance, wisdom, energy, decline, and cessation all take place by themselves within the universal subtle law. It is incorrect to say that any of these must be achieved through external effort.

"Kind prince, if one insists on the conditions under which things develop and searches for the causes thereof, such searching and insistence will never end until one comes to something that is unconditional. Then the principles of self-transformation will become clear.

"There are those who say that the semishadow penumbra is conditioned by the shadow, the shadow by the body, and the body by the creator. However, the creator is uncreated and all forms materialize by themselves, just as the great Tai Chi is 'self-so.' Throughout the entire realm of existence, one will see that there is nothing, not even the semi-shadow, that does not transform itself beyond the phenomenal world. Hence, everything creates itself through the integration of yin and yang, without the direction of any creator. Since all things create themselves, they are self-determined. This is the immortal model of the universe.

"Kind prince, there is not a single thing in the universe that has been accomplished. There is also not one thing that is unaccomplished. The 'accomplished' is called the phase of stillness and rigidity; the 'unaccomplished,' the phase of dynamics and flexibility. The still phenomenon is called yin, and the dynamic phenomenon is called yang. The yang is always pushing itself forward, looking for accomplishment, while the yin is always receptive to joining yang and continuing the process of accomplishment. The integration of yin and yang is called Tai Chi.

"Everything that exists is an expression of Tai Chi. Every small particle is a Tai Chi. The vast universe is a Tai Chi. A single event is a Tai Chi. The gathering of small events or units is a Tai Chi. The dispersion of the vast universe is a Tai Chi. There is nothing beyond Tai Chi or excluded from it. Thus, the individual body is a Tai Chi. The cosmic body is also a Tai Chi. Tai Chi is the integral truth of the universe."

~· 40 ·~

"Venerable Teacher," said the prince, "now it is completely clear to me: the path of subtle integration of the living universe operates behind all phenomena and penetrates even the smallest particles of substance. Substance is merely the condensation of energy; everything in the universe is an expression of the subtle path and universal law that permeates all time and space. Nothing can evade it. The subtle law is as natural and essential as breathing. Just as when people stop breathing they violate the normalcy of the body, when anything violates the subtle law, there is immediate disaster.

"There is a natural order of things which cannot be violated or dismissed. Food, for example, is eaten through the mouth, not the nostrils, and we see through our eyes, not our ears. Everything has its natural function with which one cannot argue. Functions are many and varied, but they all serve nature.

"At first, one may be ignorant of the subtle path because one is aware of particular phenomena rather than the subtle connection between what he thinks and says and does and what appears in his universe. When a person becomes aware of this connection, he may begin to cultivate himself in order to align his life with the subtle order of universal life. As he develops, he gradually discovers that all things are subtly connected through the cosmic body, but at this stage cosmic law is still perceived as one thing and his own being as another. Often such a person feels troubled, because he thinks the subtle law confines him and that he is at its mercy. This is because he still entertains the notion of self and sees the subtle law as something external to himself. His desires fight his mind, his mind fights his spirit, and he is in a constant state of conflict and turmoil, both within himself and with the world around him. He may struggle throughout his whole lifetime. If, however, the struggle motivates him to further cultivate himself, to disperse his desires and cleanse the obscurity of his mind, it gradually dawns on him that he and the subtle path are one. There is no separation. He is not the isolated individual he thought himself to be. All divine, subtle beings, all enlightened beings are one with him. What happiness one experiences in that state of consciousness!

"Yet, in reality, there is nothing called happiness nor anything called unhappiness. The concepts of happiness and unhappiness are creations of the dualistic mind; neither of them exist in the integral realm. When one is in the integral realm, Heaven and Earth and the myriad things are like one's own fingers. The physical universe is like the palm of one's hand. When all truth is manifest within oneself, there is a profound serenity that no one else can reach. Only the one who tastes it knows it.

"There is no one who can pass judgment on another person. Each individual is the master of his own life and death, the master of mortality and eternal life. What he does is what he is. This is the spiritual truth. Profound truth is always simple, yet the integral being does not call it either simple or profound."

~·41·~

"Kind prince, if someone says that the Integral One denies the reality of self and others or of life and death, what do you think? Does this person understand what the Integral One says?"

"No, Venerable Teacher, the person does not understand. The Integral One says that to affirm the notions of self and others, life and death, is equal to denying these notions, for both are merely points of view, definable concepts which can be comprehended by the mind through images and speech. All relative mental creations and conditions of life, whether ideological, pragmatic, or theological, are merely dreams, delusions, bubbles, and shadows which last no longer than the early morning dew or summer lightning in the sky. All manipulations of the mind are totally futile. The relative mind creates only conflict, both within itself and with others. One notion fights another notion; one time fights another time; life becomes full of contradiction, misery, and tragedy."

The master said, "Kind prince, an integral being does nothing to fragment his mind. He dissolves all delusions with his integral awareness."

~· 42 ·~

"Kind prince, what do you think? Are the world of ideas and the real world one and the same or are they two different worlds?"

"Venerable Teacher," replied the prince, "there is no such thing as a world of ideas. The world of ideology is merely a distorted reflection of the mind. It is a mental delusion, a deviation from the real world. When one keeps one's mind simple, undistracted, and unconditioned, the double vision of the mind is soon dissolved. Then one can see the one moon again. There is no mystery about this."

"Kind prince," continued the master, "there is nothing in the realm of ideas that is absolute and because of this, all efforts to form ideologies are ultimately futile. Only by dissolving the mind can one connect with the one great universal life.

"In reality, everything is integral, because the Universal Way is the only way that exists. Duality is merely an illusory product of the mind. In order to perceive the integral reality of the universe, it is necessary to transcend the mental process of separation and fragmentation. For one who has transcended duality, there is only the Universal Way of life. Because the Universal Way of life exists, it is possible to transcend the dualistic mind.

"The integral mind knows that there is no self, that everything is One Self; thus it understands that if one does something outwardly to others, one in fact has done it inwardly to oneself. Every being is the center of his own universe, his own conjoint reality, and everything about him is one element which composes his conjoint world."

～· 43 ·～

"Kind prince, there is great power in an integrated and sincere mind. By keeping their minds whole and untouched, the ancient sages evolved profound mental and spiritual abilities. They understood that intellectual development by itself fragments the mind and can lead a person far from the true nature of life. In the future, humanity will overemphasize the intellectual element of the mind. Instead of recognizing the wholeness of life, people will perceive life as having a worldly aspect and a spiritual aspect that are separate and unrelated to each other. People will also lose themselves in isolated fragments of conceptual information and become the victims rather than the masters of their knowledge.

"The remedy for people of the future age of great confusion lies in the ancient knowledge of the Universal

Way of life that has been passed down from generation to generation. The holistic way of life practiced by the very ancient sages incorporated body, mind, and spirit as a whole in all activities. Their clothing, diet, and dwellings were in accord with nature. They relied on their limbs for transportation. Their education was broad and comprehensive; it did not emphasize one element of their being while neglecting the others. They did not seek out special activities for recreation; their work and recreation were one and the same. Their forms of exercise developed not only the body, but the mind and spirit as well through the harmonization of their internal energies. Their music functioned as a bridge of communication between mind and spirit and was not just an emotional release. Their leaders were chosen because they were outstanding models of virtue, not for their financial or military capabilities. Philosophy, science, and spiritual practice were incorporated as one whole.

"Kind prince, an individual's true growth occurs in the process of solving the problems of life. All difficulties can be resolved through following the holistic, integral way of life."

The prince replied, "Venerable Teacher, how can people in the future era of confusion deal with their greatly troubled times?"

"Kind prince, the people of the future should not blindly accept the new nor blindly reject the old. Things that were developed long ago may still have great value if they have been proven safe and effective by the test of time. The new inventions that will appear may seem to be short cuts, but things of temporal convenience will bring hidden troubles later. Future generations will need to re-evaluate all old and new discoveries and inventions to ensure that they are useful and healthy, according to the standards of a holistic way of life."

"Venerable Teacher, how does one recognize the Universal Way?"

"Kind prince, one recognizes the Universal Way and reaches the highest level of personal spiritual development through the effort of searching and the continual process of refinement. Because one's own developed spiritual capability is the better pilot of one's lifeboat, some may call this the Universal Way, yet the Universal Way is not a discovery or established doctrine. Never be so childish as to think that one may concentrate on spiritual cultivation and moral discipline without making oneself virtuously useful by serving others. This kind of attitude is either a psychological illness or a childish game that trades religious devotion for psychological protection and transient emotional blessings."

~· 44 ·~

"Kind prince," said the master, "those who are motivated to attain awareness of the integral truth should follow the way discussed in this sacred record in order to perceive, to know, and to understand both the internal and the external. They should not be fooled by the false images of the mind. Attachment to the false images of the mind is the greatest obstacle to reaching awareness of the integral truth of the universe.

"Kind prince, to believe in the reality of images is equal to believing in the unreality of images. Both are mere concepts which separate one from direct intuitional contact with the integral truth. To know the truth is to know nothing, yet when one knows the truth, there is nothing one is not aware of.

"To have whole vision is to have no vision of anything in particular, yet there is nothing which can escape one's discernment. People who are unenlightened have not yet reached the integral truth, for they cannot direct their mental energy to flow in the right channel. Instead, they adhere to totally false, rigidly formed belief systems that are composed of concepts derived from the limited sensory organs. This distorted information is stored and arranged by the memory and judgment systems. Thus, the more one knows and understands, the more dimness and confusion are created. One is continually bewildered by what one knows and sees. If, by chance, one manages to avoid falling into the pitfall of the content of what one knows and sees, one invariably becomes trapped in the mechanics of how one knows and sees. If one is not confused by the appearance of what one sees, then one can be fooled by what enables one to see. The mind clings to the false images it creates. All of this conditioning builds up layer upon layer of conceptual filters through which one then looks at the world. Thus, not only is one's perception of the world distorted by the interposition of these false images, but one's very being becomes distorted. This adds further hindrance to reaching the integral truth.

"Kind prince, this is why it only aggravates the situation further to do anything to eliminate the vexation of the mind. In the process of working to eliminate mental vexation, more trouble and further separation are created. This prevents one from getting in touch with one's true being and from moving forward toward the integral reality of the universe. The movement created by the attempt to eliminate mental vexation, such as turning to religion for help or escape, is just another deviation from the correct channel in which one's mental energy should flow. If, at this moment, one does not become attached to what one sees and knows, one can uncover one's true insight and thereby see through the illusory situations of life. Actually, attachment is the separation from the wholeness of truth. Theological promises, the appearance of life and death, and all human activities are fruitless compared to the integral truth. When one dissolves the illusion of separation from the source of the Universal Mind, one restores one's own original, pure mind. It is the accumulation of dust and dirt, gathered while living in the world, that prevents one from truly experiencing the fullness of life. Once the dust and dirt are cleansed away, one suddenly becomes brilliantly illuminated with the awareness of integral unity. It is not by creation or design that one can enjoy awareness of oneness with the subtle cosmic body, but only through the direct experience of the Universal Way of life. Nor can one experience the Universal Way of life by fastening oneself to anything the mind creates, but only by following the Universal Way can one see and know correctly. Clarity and enlightenment are brought about without one's having to move an inch, for the integral truth is always found within one's own true nature."

～· 45 ·～

The master continued his instruction. "Because the mind is the central aspect of a human being, the rectification of the mind in turn rectifies all of one's life activities so that they flow in one appropriate channel. The Universal Way of life does not entail adding something to oneself; it depends on decreasing something. One eliminates the yin elements of one's life while nurturing and developing the yang elements. The following is a guideline for all life in the relative realm:

- Eliminate the habitual, clinging tendency of consciousness and instead keep the mind detached and whole.
- Eliminate all illusions and delusions and instead maintain true awareness.
- Eliminate scattered and dissipating mental activities and concentrate instead on the purity of the unconditioned mind.
- Eliminate all mental obscurity, and instead embrace crystal clarity.

- Eliminate confused dreams and daydreams in order to protect and refine one's inner vision.
- Eliminate disturbed emotion in order to return to serenity.

"Kind prince, in reality there is nothing to eliminate and nothing to establish. People deviate from their true nature and thus feel the need to do something to rectify their deviation, yet the more they do the farther they stray from their true nature. When one worships an idol or an image or an idea, it is like trying to wash water or creating a new head to put on top of the head one already has. Such activities merely add to people's restlessness. When people stop such restless activity, their integrity is spontaneously there. The solution lies in nondoing."

~· 46 ·~

"Venerable Teacher," began the wise prince, "I now understand that all ideas, thoughts, knowledge, and emotional reactions are totally empty. There is not one single thing in life that can be held as the final and complete truth. One should not be preoccupied with the trivialities of life, therefore, but should dedicate oneself to the immutable truth of integral Oneness."

"Kind prince, the Unnamable gives birth to One: a single phenomenon. The One gives birth to Two: the single phenomenon divides itself in two. The Two give birth to Three, for there must be something between every polarity. And the Three give birth to myriad things. All things are embodied by yin and embrace yang as their essential core.

"The Five Subtle Phases are the parallel evolutionary movement of all phenomena. Everything in the universe can be categorized according to the Eight Great Manifestations.

"Kind prince, if anyone holds the One, he must neglect the Two. If he holds the Two, he must neglect the Three. If he holds the Three, he must neglect the myriad things. Each stage of development is the reality of the universe, yet one cannot hold one stage as the complete reality. Therefore, kind prince, ignore the One, the Two, the Three, and the myriad things. Do not take a part as the whole, because a part is not the whole. Do not take the whole as the whole, because any part is the whole."

"Venerable Teacher, I understand that I should have no attachment to anything, either the absolute or the relative, either the One or the myriad things."

"Kind prince, holding 'no attachment' as truth is still a deviation from the truth. When one rejects one side to hold another, one is still in the relative realm. One's mind should be like a smooth pearl rolling on a very even disc; it should move without the slightest interruption or stagnation. Moving is normal, stagnation is sickness."

"Venerable Teacher, I shall be very glad when I reach the stage where my mind is as refined as a pearl and my life experience is like an even disc."

"Kind prince, get rid of the images of the pearl and the disc, for they are not real. When one appears, the other appears, and when one disappears, the other also disappears. What can be called the mind? What can be called the experience? There is nothing which can be called the 'pearl-like mind' or 'disc-like experience'; they are merely conditions. So-called pain and happiness are merely conditions as well, and if one dissolves one's ego, what can be called pain and what misfortune? What can be called happiness and what good fortune?

"Kind prince, when one establishes the One, then there must be Two. When Two are established, there must be Three. When Three have been established, there must be myriad things and then you have all kinds of divergence and diversity. Therefore, kind prince, to dissolve the One is to dissolve the myriad things. The way to unite the diversity is not to search for unity. Forget about searching for Oneness; do not bother to harmonize anything. The universe is already harmonious. Followers of religion are always looking for inner peace, but they lose their inner peace in searching for it."

"Venerable Teacher, I deeply appreciate your profound teaching on spiritual self-evolution. I completely comprehend that this great teaching is of the mental sphere, yet I cannot ignore the reality of life, of nature, and of the universe."

"Kind prince, the total subtle reality is unnamable, indescribable, and unthinkable; however, this does not mean that it cannot be known. It is merely unknowable to the conceptual mind; it is beyond thinking and language. The innate faculties of intuition and insight cannot be put into namable, describable terms. Intuition knows the whole; intellect knows only fragments. People tend to develop only one aspect of the mind; this is hazardous and causes imbalance. Stop chiseling away the wholeness of the mind. All truth is there. All happiness in life is there."

"Venerable Teacher, I will cultivate wholeness of mind and develop my intuition and insight as the ultimate cultivation."

"Kind prince, there is no need to develop anything. Take away the weeds and the crop will grow naturally by itself. The purpose of self-cultivation is natural self-transformation. You do not need to weed out the hindrances; to do so is to create more hindrances. All that is necessary is to maintain serenity, yet serenity is not the final goal.

"All the principles of nature are contained within the wholeness of an individual's vision. These principles are the Subtle Path, the polarizing movement between the unmanifest and the manifest, the cyclic pattern of all changes, the Five Subtle Phases as the self-balancing function of nature, and the Eight Great Manifestations as the general categories of all phenomena. The intuitional vision of an individual does not exclude nature. One uses nature to intuit nature; one uses nature to restore and evolve nature. All truth is contained in Tai Chi, and Tai Chi is everything; there is nothing beyond it. The truth of cultivating the mind is to balance its polarities. The same truth also applies to the cultivation of the body and spirit.

Learning this way, people will be able to achieve world peace.

"The great secret of immortal cultivation and the harmonious universe is expressed in the Tai Chi symbol (☯). Even so-called self-nature cannot hold on to it. Everything takes something from something else. The basic structure of the universe that is generally recognized as time and space is not something solid. Time and space can change and dissolve, but the existence of a being or thing does not rely on the framework of time and space. Time and space have no self-nature. They are only accessories of an event, a thing, or a being. Nonbeing does not mean that something does not really exist, but that it exists beyond the senses, time, and space. Supernatural beings extend their life force freely to the lives of form and non-form and at the same time keep themselves unformed and supernatural. Is the supernatural something separate from the reality of nature? Wise prince, these two realities can be discussed separately, but both sides belong to the same substance of the great, one universal life. The subtle law of integral life emphasizes neither the natural nor the supernatural. In the process of human evolution, the integral truth is reached by one who is whole and who is not entrapped by natural or supernatural phenomena."

~ 47 ~

"Kind prince, the way of dualistic worldly life is unhealthy; the way of misleading religions is distorted; the way of materialism is cruel; the way of blind spiritualization is unreal. Chanting is not more holy than the murmuring of a stream. Counting one's prayer beads is not more sacred than normal breathing. Colorful religious robes are not more spiritual than plain civilian clothes. Therefore, relying on these superficial trappings of spiritual life will get one nowhere. The only way to attain the absolute state of being is through embracing absolute Oneness and leading a selfless life. By anonymously contributing to others' lives one may burnish the brightness of one's soul and radiate virtue to the world. Imbalance may be created by overdeveloping the physical or mental aspects of one's being. Be calm, happy, and content with your own being and live only according to your true nature.

"Kind prince, it is impossible to escape the destiny you have formed by your past actions. There is hope, however, for evolving and transforming one's being. Those who have all-encompassing, integral awareness are able to take responsibility for their lives and for their environment. They radiate a healthy influence to others and illuminate the world's darkness. Their absolute virtue becomes a sanctuary, not only for themselves, but for all beings. Virtue is the only true power of life. Those on the Integral Way are resolutely dedicated to their own evolution and also to the evolution of all beings. Their lives are a process of self-refinement and self-transcendence. They are truly an extension of the Integral One."

∽·48·∽

"Venerable Teacher," said the prince, "I now understand that there are two approaches to true spiritual cultivation. One is the affirmative approach which accepts and includes everything with a positive attitude. From an ethical point of view, it means extending universal virtue to all, regardless of any external condition. This is different from the relative, affirmative attitude that is expounded by religions and which includes some things or people and excludes others. According to the Universal Way, the affirmative approach excludes nothing.

"The other approach to spiritual cultivation involves the denial of all things external to one's own true nature. This includes the denial of all creations, all individuality, and all conditions. Only by denying these things can you unveil and unfold layer after layer of illusion. Finally, after all the layers have been peeled away, one comes to see the integral, universal truth.

"This may seem paradoxical, but the attitudes of affirmation and denial amount to the same thing. We accept all and deny all at the same time. If you deny all that is external to your true nature, you eliminate all mental entanglement and contamination and thereby raise your spirit and achieve crystal clarity. But the same thing happens by accepting all things without any partiality toward one particular thing. Both aspects are equally important, like the right and the left hands. In this way, yin and yang assist each other in order to transcend duality and achieve integral awareness.

"All of a person's viewpoints, concepts about life, and religious convictions are a manifestation of his energy. If one's mind is strongly conditioned, it is as if one measures everything with a crooked ruler; he can never measure anything accurately. If one's aim, however, is to know the truth, then one must straighten and refine one's measuring instrument, for if the instrument is faulty, one cannot perceive reality precisely.

"When the nervous system of a human being is restored and refined, one becomes calm and objective. One can then see clearly and discover that although there is diversity in the universe, there is unity behind that diversity. One may intellectually learn, understand, and accept the unity of the universe, but this is very different from arriving at the unity through personal spiritual purification. Struggling to achieve unity is not as natural as the spontaneous experience of and participation in unity itself. One cannot perceive the unity of the universe in terms of subject and object and still call it unity."

"Kind prince," said the master, "to the Integral One there is nothing to call unity and nothing to call diversity. There is nothing to call subject and nothing to call object. These are merely labels created by the dualistic mind."

~ 49 ~

"Venerable Teacher, I am now deeply aware that to know or think about something is much different than actually aligning oneself with the reality of being and doing it. To have a quick mind or tongue is not equal to real achievement. A person may think he is a good rider, but once he takes up the horse's reins, it takes time and practice in order to ride well. To talk and think about the Universal Way is merely talking and thinking, which do not go beyond the relative realm; to an integral being, talking and thinking are irrelevant. The Universal Way is not just a matter of speaking wisdom, but one of continual practice in order to reach a universal realization. If one hopes to align oneself with it, one must practice it. If one does not practice it, one will never reach it. Although it takes years of practice to become one with the Universal Way, it takes but an instant to realize it."

"Kind prince," said the master, "just relax your body and quiet your senses. Forget that you are one among many. Undo the mind and allow it to return to its virgin purity. Loosen the spirits within you. Thus all things return to their root, and because there is no separation between them and their source, their return goes unrecognized. To know of the return is to depart from it. Do not be curious about its name and do not be in awe of its forms. Then the truth will present itself to you naturally of itself and you will join in oneness with deep and boundless reality. This is what it means to be an Integral One."

~· 50 ·~

"Kind prince," continued the master, "one is what one does. Behavior which is motivated by any kind of external pressure or internal impulse is not the straight expression of one's true nature. The only genuine behavior is that which is a direct expression of one's true, virtuous nature. When all of one's behavior is an extension of one's true nature, one may be called a natural, integral being.

"Natural, integral beings are the immortals of the universe. They never violate their true nature and thus are able to endure eternally. They are not like mortal beings who follow what is variable instead of what is invariable.

"Kind prince, what do you think? Should a person expend all of his vitality in order to actively accumulate more material things than he could possibly use in a lifetime? Should he do all kinds of good deeds in order to gather blessings in the next life? Or should he cultivate himself so that he may live in the spiritual realm? How much regard should he pay to the practical aspects of life?"

The prince humbly bowed to the master and said, "Venerable Teacher, according to the integral model you have established for all beings to follow, it is clear that one should live wholly and virtuously, following the Universal Way of life and making no discrimination between what is spiritual and what is mundane, what is present, past, or future; ignoring all relative concepts, one should embrace only the immutable Oneness."

~ 51 ~

The master continued, "Kind prince, when one attains awareness of the subtle integral truth, one is able to comprehend all aspects of one's life. To realize the constancy and steadiness in your life is to realize the deep nature of the universe. This realization is not dependent on any transitory internal or external condition, rather it is an expession of one's own immutable spiritual nature. The only way to attain the Universal Way is to maintain the integral virtues of constancy, steadiness, and simplicity in one's daily life.

"There are four cardinal virtues which assist one in achieving this goal. The first is unconditional natural piety. Natural piety means love and respect for one's being, both the internal aspects and the external manifestations. Unconditional natural piety is very different from the artificial, blind piety advocated by religions; it is a state of profound reverence toward natural life. People of later generations will need to restore this natural reverence which is arrived at through the rejection of all false images and concepts. When one's mind has been liberated from its bondage to illusion, one is spontaneously aware of the true sacredness of one's life in the universe. It is no longer necessary to create an external belief as the object of one's reverence, for one's own being and everything in one's environment are seen as divine in and of themselves.

"The second virtue is natural sincerity. To be naturally sincere means to be genuine, earnest, honest, and wholehearted. To be naturally sincere also means being free of all self-deception. To have no self-deception means to embrace the divine nature of life. Integral virtue among natural people is the integral nature of the universe. To be naturally sincere means to keep one's mind whole, unfragmented, and centered. The distorted mind always suffers because it constantly creates separation and dichotomy, preventing real peace within. Keeping one's mind whole and at ease will not only assure inner peace so that one may transcend all transient trivialities, but it also reconnects one with the deep and constant nature of the universe.

"The third virtue is gentleness. When one is rough, one tends to be aggressive, inconsiderate, and unkind to others. This behavior inevitably rebounds on oneself. When one is rough, one is also insensitive to the subtle truth of the universe. Roughness can lead to the destruction of one's connection with the spiritual realms, for the level of gentleness of one's being is the level of refinement of one's soul, and the more gentle and subtle one's energy, the closer one is to union with the subtle truth of the universe.

"The fourth virtue is being naturally supportive. This means that one does not set his mind to do only what he likes all the time, but in his spare time he helps others for positive purposes. To be a spiritual teacher or worker is to achieve oneself by serving others without reservation. Such virtue may take many years to develop through cultivating a skill or talent or wealth to a point where one can afford to serve without expecting anything big in return. Through serving others, one can find dignity and the true meaning of life.

"These four virtues are not an external standard or dogma, but attributes of one's true nature which is referred to as Chen or natural sincerity. These four virtues can give birth to all other virtues, the greatest of which are: Jen, or impersonal love for all living things; I, (pronounced *ee*) or propriety, rectitude, and faithfulness in expressing natural friendliness; Li, or moderation, self-restraint, and nonaggression; Tse, or wisdom; and Sheng, or being reliable and trustworthy.

"All virtues lead to true blessings. The five greatest blessings are: Fuh, or happiness that makes no demands; Su, or longevity that does not make things short; Kang, or health that is free from abuse; Ning, or peace that is not self-disturbing or disturbing to others; and Fui, or wealth that does not come about through scheming. Virtue is the mother of all blessings, for it not only brings forth blessings but also protects them.

"An integral being's positive attitude toward life is based on his correct awareness. He lives every moment of his life with virtue, thus every moment of his life is rightly accomplished. Living in this manner, one is free from any regret. The lives of those who achieve awareness of the integral oneness of the universe are models of virtue for the entire world."

"Venerable Teacher, I have been taught that a mind which is free of preconception is an empty mind. I understand that to practice empty-mindedness does not mean suspending all thought, but rather keeping one's mind as clear as a cloudless sky. In this case, should one practice positive and creative thinking?"

"Kind prince, one should frequently empty one's mind by clearing away all confusion, disorder, and dichotomy. This cleansing process is similar to using a basin full of water to wash a baby. After the baby is washed, the dirty water should be discarded, yet one should not discard the baby with the bath water. The individual who practices the cessation of thought in order to become a superbeing is like one who discards the baby with the bath water. It is incorrect to practice empty-mindedness without reaching whole-mindedness as a positive virtue of life."

"Venerable Teacher, should one spend all of his time and energy in quiet sitting meditation in order to remain above all worldly conditions and maintain empty-mindedness?"

"Kind prince, one who spends all of his time and energy in quiet sitting meditation for this purpose is only fixing his mind in a certain, narrow way. This is not empty-mindedness, but only narrow-mindedness. Such practice does not lead one anywhere, much less to becoming an integrally virtuous being.

"The practice of whole-mindedness, you see, is not the practice of stiffness. What is stiff belongs in the company of the dead, whereas what is supple belongs in the company of the living. The mind should be like water that is always flowing smoothly. One should not designate a specific time or place in which to practice empty-mindedness, but should practice mental unassertiveness in all aspects of life, the essential as well as the trivial."

The prince replied, "Venerable Teacher, should one intentionally and completely avoid all worldly troubles and activities for the purpose of practicing simplicity and keeping the mind clear?"

"Kind prince, if there were no worldly troubles and activities, how could one practice simplicity? Simplicity is the key to handling the troubles and activities of daily life. It is the deep reality of all natural and human matters, while the manifold forms are the events. Looking to the single essence to govern events is the meaning of simplicity in the practical sense."

"Venerable Teacher," asked the prince, "how should one practice integral virtue in daily life?"

"Kind prince, to have integral virtue is to have unchangeable virtue. In daily life, one should fulfill one's obligations in the five great relationships. As a parent, one should love one's children. As a son or daughter, one should abide by one's parents' deep wish for one to live a decent, healthy life. As a subordinate, one should carry out one's positive duty unfailingly with a sense of cooperation and teamwork. As a superior, one should assume full responsibility without blaming one's subordinates as an excuse. As a brother or sister, one should extend love and help to the younger ones, and the younger ones should do the same for the older ones. As a friend, one should be faithful. As a husband or wife, one should devotedly care for one's mate. In general, one should carry out any work that comes to one with righteousness. One should be concerned with making one's best contribution rather than seeking unrightful promotion and personal profit. One should practice steadfast and indiscriminative virtue without demanding others to do the same in return. These mental attitudes are the manifestation of such virtue."

"Venerable Teacher, what are the characteristics of one who is spiritually mature?"

"Kind prince, one who is spiritually mature is not a follower of dualistic religion. Most of the world's people worship the offspring, while one who is spiritually mature embraces the Source and never becomes the slave of any social or religious movement. He considers the world his family and accepts all people as his brothers and sisters. He offers his service to all and asks no recompense. He has broken through all perceptual obstructions and can see through all the diverse names which create discrimination and hostility, yet he respects natural variety and differences and treats all things as equal. He guards his life and the lives of others from negative destruction and does not foster unhealthy prosperity. He knows all the tricks of human beings, yet practices steadfast virtues.

He has achieved awareness of the totality of truth, yet he maintains a simple, matter-of-fact manner. He may achieve supernatural abilities, yet he leads a plain life. He will be at the height of human spiritual achievement, yet he remains indistinguishable from ordinary people."

The prince then said, "Venerable Teacher, can one be complete if one practices universal heartedness and universal mindedness without learning the holistic, Universal Way of life?"

"Kind prince, universal heartedness and universal mindedness are the Universal Way of life. There is only one Universal Way, but from different perspectives it is given different names."

"Venerable Teacher, I will practice the Universal Way of life with great joy and pass it on to all spiritual descendants so that it will be preserved generation after generation."

"Kind prince, the one who practices the Universal Way shall be greatly blessed."

⌐ 53 ⌐

"Venerable Teacher, the instruction you have transmitted to us is rare and supreme guidance from the highest realm. You have led us to the Universal Way and taught us how to realize our own complete virtue. Your disciples, however, still dwell in the relative realm and are subject to the forces of yin and yang and the five subtle phases of energy. Would you teach us how we may use these forces to serve others and develop ourselves?"

"Kind prince," replied the master, "a person may learn to be completely virtuous, but if he is unable to serve others, or if his usefulness is limited by the fact that he himself needs help, then he cannot be said to be completely virtuous. A truly virtuous person cannot be indifferent to the troubled world in which he lives and must develop skills and methods by which to help himself and others. It is essential to understand that the truth of wholeness has two main attributes: substance and function. The substance is called Ti, the body or prime principle. The function is called Yun, or usefulness. Together they are a complete Tai Chi and serve as the two wings which can carry one to the integral realm. When this principle is applied to yin and yang, yin may be considered as the substance and yang the function, or vice versa. Ti and Yun are mutually dependent; in the deepest sense, substance is function and function is substance.

"During the three ancient generations of Fu Hsi, Sheng Nung, and Huang Ti (the period of history prior to 2700 BCE), people did not need to do anything in order to be sages. They practiced 'nonpartial doingness and mindedness' and were naturally wise. Later, after this era had passed, people began to deviate from the integrity and virtue of originalness and it became necessary for them to practice self-cultivation in order to restore their wholeness and originalness. This restoration is referred to as the attainment of self-awareness. It corresponds with Ti, the substance of Tao, which enables people to reach the divine origin of nonmaking. In order to complete the

Tai Chi, however, it is necessary for those who have attained Ti to also extend Yun, the function of Tao. This may happen through any constructive profession, business, or activity. Only one who embodies both Ti and Yun can be called a man or woman of Tao.

"The interdependence of Ti and Yun is illustrated in the following story. A blind man and a lame man shared the same dwelling, and one day a cinder flew out of the fireplace. Within a short time the entire house was in flames. Each man tried separately to escape, but neither could get out of the house. Finally the blind man said to the lame man, 'You have eyes and I have legs. If you climb on my back, you can direct me to the door.' In a few moments they were safely outside."

"Venerable Teacher," said the prince, "it is my sincere intention to become the embodiment of both Ti and Yun by cultivating crystal-clear awareness of the integral truth and extending unconditional virtue to the world."

~·54·~

"Kind prince, your sincerity has moved me to reveal to you the tool which will enable you to realize your virtuous being. There are several categories of holistic subtle sciences which are vehicles for serving others and assisting one's own spiritual evolution. Within each category are hundreds of thousands of details which may be learned. It is not necessary to know all of them in order to reach the integral realm, however, one may make good use of them in one's life and for the benefit of others.

"Some of these holistic sciences were discovered through the spiritual unfolding of highly evolved beings who lived on earth during very ancient times. Others were developed through the power of intuition and the ability to link one's mind with the Universal Mind. Generation after generation, these methods have been passed down from highly evolved beings to virtuous individuals who are in the process of spiritual evolution to assist them in developing their spirit and intuition. If an individual does not develop his spirit and intuition, it is impossible to make full use of these techniques and this information to evolve to his fullest potential.

"This profound guidance is transmitted by a teacher of this esoteric tradition according to the disciple's personal needs and his or her potential for development. Since very ancient times, it has been strictly prohibited to teach some of the mystical knowledge and methods to the unvirtuous. For this reason, those who have achieved a certain level of development may discover, study, and research these methods by themselves as evidence of their spiritual unfolding. Those methods and subjects which are most practical should be developed and disseminated to the general public. All of the valuable, ancient methods should be preserved, protected, and continually developed by people of high virtue in future generations. Those who, because of intellectual prejudice, disregard this wisdom will cause the setback of human cultural development and spiritual evolution. This will mark the beginning of humanity's great difficulty.

"Kind prince, those who guide themselves and others with clear awareness illuminate the darkness of the world."

∽ 55 ∽

The master continued, "Kind prince, the holistic, subtle sciences of the ancient sages are an integration of science, art, and personal spiritual development. The practice of these methods employs the laws of nature and the subtle realm and involves the participation of body, mind, and spirit as an integral whole.

"I will mention a few of the subjects that comprise this system. For instance, there are:

1. The holistic science of healing, referred to as Yi Yau. Yi means healing, while *Yau* means seeking, preparing, and using medicinal materials. This science is a complete system of diagnosis, acupuncture, herbology, therapeutic diet, and other healing techniques. The ancient developed ones, with their developed mental and spiritual faculties, discovered medicinal herbal plants and found that there were certain points on the surface of the body which are connected to the internal organs and specific body systems and which become tender when a person is ill. When the illness goes away so does the tenderness. They developed very advanced techniques of manipulat-

ing these points to influence the internal organs and systems. This is how acupuncture and acupressure were originally developed. Through their deep insight, the ancient sages also discovered that diagnosis could be made by observing a person's aura, his eyes and ears, tongue, pulse waves, voice, and movement, as well as the specific symptoms of disease. The ability to correctly diagnose depends on the healer's personal achievement through training, spiritual self-cultivation and intuitional error-free response.

2. The holistic science of foreknowledge of an individual's destiny, referred to as Syang Ming. *Syang* means observing, while *Ming* means all the interrelated aspects of an individual's life. The ancient sages observed that outward physical manifestations of a person's face, bone structure, palms, and voice revealed corresponding inner attitudes and that one's destiny could be seen in those corresponding energy patterns. The natural and subtle influences on an individual's life could be predicted by employing the system of the five subtle phases of energy which occur in regular patterns in time and space.

3. The holistic science of the influence of subtle universal energy rays on specific geographic locations, referred to as Feng Shui, or geomancy, originated when ancient developed ones needed to locate a safe spot for building houses, towns, etc. Different physical locations on earth have different energy rays and are thus beneficial for

different kinds of use or structures. The ability to discern these different rays and their various potencies and to understand how they can support various purposes was greatly valued. Less developed practitioners may not truly know these things by simply observing the operation of the five subtle phases of energy in nature.

4. The holistic science of foreknowledge for specific purposes by arranging and observing the subtle alternations of yin and yang, referred to as Fu Kua, the Inquiry of Changing Signs. The ancient sages revealed all the possible combinations of yin and yang in a system called the *I Ching*, or Book of Changes. They discovered that by throwing coins, seeds, or yarrow sticks in a prescribed manner, one could arrive at a specific arrangement of yin and yang which would comment on a question asked. In this way, one could determine the consequences of particular events expressed in a symbolic picture. By observing the balance of yin and yang changes, good decisions could be made regarding military action or the events of daily life. The purpose of practicing the I Ching is to learn the balance of movement without following one's impulses toward an extreme and without becoming intellectually assertive. This is a good system for training people to make decisions that are harmonious with the apparent and latent aspects of any situation and to consider the short and long term effects of their actions. Practically speaking, no one should rigidly

hold on to the guidance they receive from the I Ching, but should value instead the philosophy of balance in individual life as well as great events.

5. The holistic science of sublimating and refining personal energy for the purpose of revitalization and rejuvenation. To accomplish the integration of both sides of different souls of an individual, two schools developed. One way is working to achieve immortality through internal efforts; this is the science referred to as Nei Dan, or the Inner Immortal Medicine, the holistic science of external alchemy for the refinement of golden immortal elixir through the use of rare and undecaying materials. This science is referred to as Wai Dan, or External Immortal Medicine, which has brought forth the development of modern chemistry and further advances in alchemy. The other way is to obtain the golden immortal elixir through single or dual cultivation. This science is also referred to as Nei Dan, or the Inner Immortal Medicine, which can fortify a person's soul if correctly guided. Usually, people are taught only the holistic science of sexual education for the purpose of enhancing one's health and enjoyment and for balancing one's emotions, referred to as Fang Jung, or the Healthy Way of the Inner Room. This is at a different level than what I have described as Internal Medicine. What is popularly known as tantra originated from this practice; it is not a secret, but an education.

6. The correct way of internal alchemy is the holistic science of the mystical conception of a unified spiritual life of wholeness through specific breathing and mental techniques. This method is referred to as Tai Syi, or Womb Breathing to Revitalize the Body and Immortalize the Inner Being.

7. For the purpose of attaining a higher spiritual life, there is the holistic science of transforming spiritual essence through keeping one's thoughts in accord with the Divine Source. This is referred to as Chwun Shi, or the Deep Linking with Divine Thought for Inner Transformation.

8. Even with all of these good methods, one cannot neglect the holistic science of spiritual regimen for self-cultivation, especially for the purpose of becoming attuned to the cycle of universal energy rotation through avoiding or accepting specific energy rays in daily life, referred to as Shu Ser, or Self-Cultivation and Life Discipline. This facilitates the complete spiritualization of one's being.

9. To know the specific days for gathering the abundant life energy of nature is the holistic science referred to as Bi Gu, which is fasting to refill higher energy in order to refine one's life and uplift one's spirit. It is not a negative practice of avoiding mortal food, but a way of deriving Immortal Essence from nature at certain points in the cyclical movement of different stars when they are in harmonized positions.

To assist in this, the holistic science of diet for

refining and harmonizing the body, mind, and spirit was developed. It is referred to as Fu Er, or Reinforcing Energy through Eating and Drinking.

10. There were also very powerful single cultivations such as the holistic science of embracing transcendental integral oneness in order to nourish one's mystical pearl and accomplish the mystical conception, referred to as Sau Yi, or Emerging into Integral Oneness through Spiritual Practice.

11. Then, at an easily attainable level, there is the holistic science of guiding one's physical energy through a combination of will power and physical exercises in order to gain mastery of the body, breath, internal organs, mind, and life and death. The fundamental techniques include the Yellow Emperor's Classic of Energy Guidance, T'ai Chi Ch'uan, the Eight Treasures, and related methods of meditation. This science is referred to as Tow Ying, or Inducing and Guiding Energy Flows within the Individual Body.

12. The holistic science of gathering pure and high natural energy in order to reform and refine one's being with food and herbs, referred to as Fu Chi, or the Input of Vital Natural Energy, is a highly helpful approach.

13. Single external practice is not more effective than uniting both the inner and outer being. The holistic science of inner transformation through mystical visualization, referred to as Chuan Se, or Maintaining the Thought of the Integral Realm,

can also produce practical, positive help for one's life.

14. One needs to be careful about the contact one has in life. The holistic science of purifying one's energy through ascetic practices has the purpose of cleansing one's worldly contamination and altering one's destiny. It is referred to as Dzai Jing, or Spiritual Discipline and Prohibition. Doing this periodically is beneficial.

15. To further enhance one's spiritual capability, there is the holistic science of drawing mystical pictures and of writing and reciting mystical words in order to evoke a response from the subtle realm of the multileveled universe, referred to as Fu Jou, or the Science of Talismans and Invocations. These methods are used to perform exorcism, redeem souls, and subtly control rain, wind, mist, and snow.

16. For spiritual education, the holistic science of intuitional development through studying the classical scriptures and through direct training from a master's daily dialogue and contact enables one to dissolve the self and connect with the great whole. It also helps one to develop insight into all spiritual functions of the multi-universe and to harmonize with them. This method is referred to as Tsan Syan, or the Mental Search for the Mystery.

17. In order to avoid making mistakes and misjudging people one can practice the holistic science of mystical energy linkage for influencing affairs as

small as those of an individual or as great as those of a nation. It is referred to as Lyou Yen and Chi Men, the Six Primal Yang Water Energies of Mighty Wisdom and the Mystical Gates of Life and Victory. This can be a positive system for employing a very subtle arrangement of energy in order to know or change a situation of weakness or dominance in any action or nonaction. This enables people to protect themselves and their lands from invaders and to avoid becoming ruthless leaders.

"Kind prince, for beginners the common foundation of all holistic sciences is to study the *I Ching*. This could be a great means for probing both the substantial and the insubstantial spheres of life. It is an excellent training process in locating the balance point between the potential conflict of any two sides. It also develops one's ability to handle practical affairs and fosters the evolution of one's mind and spirit. I think the positive value of the *I Ching* is still educational, especially for the complicated life activities of future generations, however, anything concerning a normal, healthy life is the subject of these holistic sciences. They are all instruments for attaining Tao, and all instruments of Tao exist to serve the wholeness of one universal life."

~· 56 ·~

The master said, "Kind prince, Tao is complete. It is like a big tree with roots, trunk, branches, twigs, leaves, flowers, and fruit. Partial practice is not the integral Tao. When one takes any single portion as the whole tree, one creates a distorted worldly religion or a fragmented worldly science. Take the human body for example; it has five senses, two groups of internal organs, four limbs with fingers and toes, etc., all comprising the whole. If one takes a finger or a limb or one of the organs as an object of study, it will create a perspective of dissected details, not the total view. The form and function of a human being come from the integration of all the parts. This is true not only in man but also in the vast multi-universe.

"Kind prince, a big tree with its roots, its trunk, its branches, twigs, flowers, and fruit, begins from a tiny seed, just as the multi-universe originates from invisible particles of energy. All forms come from the formless. The manifest is the subtle performance of the unmanifest. The unmanifest and the manifest become the root of each other as yin and yang polarities of the integral Tai Chi."

"Venerable Teacher," said the prince, "is it correct to say that everything is Tao?"

"Kind prince, everything that serves the true nature of life is Tao. Everything that does not serve the true nature of life is not Tao. In order to not mislead you I must reveal precisely that everything is Tao and everything is not Tao. To protect and hide oneself under a beautiful concept or to follow a religion and do nothing to serve the world is unvirtuous. It is a sin to enjoy oneself in a monastery all day long, thinking one is practicing holiness. To a person of Tao, everything is Tao. To a person who has disintegrated himself from Tao, everything is not Tao."

ᴖ· 57 ·ᴖ

The master continued, "There are numberless energy rays in the universe, including the rays of all the stars, life beings, and nonphysical life beings in nature. All rays and spirits come from the subtle nature of the universe, and single energy rays or groups of rays relate with and influence everything in their environment. Although these rays never take concrete form, they always exist in the subtle sphere. Without intentional design, the interwoven energy net influences the lives of individual human beings, whole societies, and entire races.

"The high energy of the Subtle Origin of the universe is unique and pure. It is absolutely positive, creative, and constructive, existing above the twisted realm of duality. The rays of stars and the potency of spirits diversify themselves from the energy ray of the Subtle Origin and interweave themselves as an intricate, subtle net in all kinds of combinations and interplay. The unintentional influence of the energy rays of the lower spheres of the universe is both positive and negative, constructive and destructive.

"A human soul is composed of various unrefined energy rays of the universe. Before an individual fully evolves to become an integral being, he may make trouble for himself and others through his unawareness. The full evolution of a human being in the relative sphere is attained through being correctly aware of how to enhance one's positive energy and eliminate subtle negative elements. Through this effort, all human beings can work for their own betterment and the development of a new life.

"A vicious individual is a being who has not yet fully evolved. While completely under the influence of the intricate energy rays and elements within and without, he may bring about disaster for himself and for his surroundings. A virtuous individual who responds to the high, pure, harmonious subtle energy rays and integrates them with the positive elements of his own inner being may strengthen his life, enhance his health and power, and lengthen his years. This is achieved through his own self-cultivation. Then, through his subtle, positive influence, he may help those who are connected with him.

"When one reconnects oneself with the ray of the Subtle Origin of the universe, one can eliminate all negative influences of the conflicting, dualistic lower spheres. The negative influence of the gross spheres of nature is an intricate combination of the energies of stars, massive objects, natural spirits and many other minor influences. Under the extensive influence of this natural force, the undeveloped human mind may be impressed with a domineering image which is like an invisible, tyrannical ruler.

This image enhances the aggressive and destructive tendencies of the undeveloped human mind and encourages it to imagine the combined forces of nature as demonic. Both of these misconceptions become strong obstacles to achieving the correct awareness necessary to enlighten a human being. Kind prince, ignore the variation of energy rays and the potency of all kinds of natural spirits. When the Universal Way is applied to one's life, they all merge into harmonious Oneness."

~· 58 ·~

"Kind prince, when an individual being or thing loses its balance, either within itself or in relationship to its external environment, its energy becomes incomplete or exhausted and eventually leads to the individual's expiration. Only divine beings have perfect equilibrium and absolute wholeness. This is why they can endure eternally. Thus, the purpose of self-cultivation is to restore the natural integration of body, mind, and spirit and to rise above being controlled by biological impulses. This is achieved by balancing yin and yang, both internally and externally, for in order to evolve to the Integral Realm, one must accomplish the indestructible integration of yin and yang."

The prince then said, "Venerable Teacher, I now understand that following an extreme theology or imbalanced ideology will lead only to partial development of one's being. Religious sects which emphasize the development of only one aspect of one's being through the rigid practice of extreme austerity, unnatural disciplines, or conforming to external dogma lead one nowhere, because these practices contradict the Universal Way of life. Very often what happens when someone tries to cultivate himself in this dichotomous manner is that either the mind becomes the traitor of the body or the body becomes the traitor of the mind. When people cultivate the mind and spirit and disregard the body, the body invariably manifests disharmony by becoming weak or sick. If the body desires sex, one may ignorantly indulge in dissipating sexual activity. If it needs food, one may make ignorant choices of food. One's behavior in these situations determines one's ideal and factual spiritual achievement.

"If the cultivation of the mind is neglected, it can become like a poisonous snake. One may hope to contain it well, like a snake in a glass cage, but it restlessly looks for a chance to escape every moment. As a result, there is no peace within most people, and this is why when a spiritual peak has been reached, no matter how many times, very few people can maintain it.

"Therefore, if a spiritual path emphasizes the partial development of one aspect of one's being while neglecting the others, its fundamental guidelines are incorrect. These spiritual paths are like helping a drunk walk home; when one side is straightened up, the person falls over to the other side, continually stumbling back and forth. One's entire being must follow one right channel in order to eliminate all contradictions within and without. With the complete cultivation and integration of body, mind, and spirit, the external world will reflect one's inner rectification and unity. One will then spontaneously manifest harmony without the need to make any demands on the external world."

"Kind prince, no spiritual peak can be maintained for long. When one experiences spiritual peaks, it is like waking up in the morning, going back to sleep at night, and then waking up again another morning. To an integral being, there is no awakening and no sleeping, no enlightenment and no darkness. A person experiences the events of life, and the experiences of life in turn reveal something about the person. When the person tries to explain the events of his life, this brings about another experience. Thus, although one may be able to describe the events of life, the direct truth of life is different from what is describable. The integral truth of the universe can hardly be put into words."

~ 59 ~

"Kind prince, the integral cultivation of immortal achievement must be built on a firm foundation of virtue. The opportunity to learn and practice such cultivation is Heaven's reward to those who are truly virtuous. All human beings are the descendants of the original spiritual inhabitants of this world many, many eons ago, but people have deviated from the accurate awareness of the divine nature of life and have lost the qualities of angelic beings. Only those who have restored the angelic qualities of their being and who have already actualized the Universal Way may be instructed in the method used by the angels to enhance and integrate their energy in order to become immortal divine beings.

"An individual cannot search for the kind of teacher who is able to instruct him in immortal cultivation, for such teachers reside in the subtle, divine realm or in seclusion where they have an ordinary appearance and lead an ordinary life. It is the teacher who seeks out the student. The experiences an individual manifests are determined by the person's inherent qualities. Therefore, if an individual is interested in receiving instruction from the divine realm regarding his spiritual evolution, he should express his virtuous qualities by extending service to the world. The immortals will then come to the one who is ready.

"Kind prince, it is important to understand that greed for enlightenment and for the secret of immortality is just as great an obstacle for those who aspire to follow the Universal Way as is greed for material wealth. Enlightenment will never come to one who covets it. Instead of desiring to attain high wisdom and know the secret of divine immortality and the mysteries of the universe, one should merely practice indiscriminative virtue. The divine immortals are watching you and guiding you at all times. When your energy is delicate enough and your virtue is powerful enough, the immortals will respond to you. One's high awareness is the true eye of one's being. When you succeed in connecting your energy with the divine realm, the immortals will dwell within you. It is not a matter of anxiously trying to obtain the utmost secrets of life. The transmission of subtle truth is the immortals' reward to the virtuous. All one needs to do is follow the Universal Way of life. Then one will naturally connect oneself with the ultimate truth of the universe. This is the way to become a responsible, fully developed, integral being and an angelic immortal of all time. This is the way all divine ones evolved to the divine realm, and it is the way all integral beings of the future will follow."

∼· 60 ·∼

"Venerable Teacher, I clearly understand now that the way to become an integral being is to eliminate all concepts of duality from the mind. An integral being can lift himself above the dusty net of worldly contamination at any time. Yin and yang are the basic principles governing the operation of the universe; there is no specific, dominant power or way. Rigid dogma, therefore, should be avoided both in the life of the individual and by rulers of the masses. Rather than engaging in worldly conflicts concerning fragments of the whole, disciples should remain impartial. This can be achieved, not by taking a neutral or indifferent stance, but by transcending the realm of duality and embracing the natural originalness.

"Dear Teacher, you have taught us that the primordial ancestors of the human race were one with the Tao and that all of their activities were in harmony with the highest subtle law, but now the worldly way and the spiritual way are no longer one; what is considered normal today was not the normalcy of the integral beings who lived in very ancient times. In what way, therefore, should your disciples cultivate themselves in order to become integral beings?"

"Kind prince," replied the master, "as one grows in self-awareness, one's being evolves from the gross to the subtle, from heavy to light. The continual refinement of personal subtle energy is the precious cultivation of immortal beings. These mystical gems of the technique of immortal achievement will be shown to the one who has completely dissolved the umbilical cord that binds him to the realm of physical energy. All students of life should devote themselves to living a virtuous, integrated life and to accomplishing the transformation of their narrow, superficial personalities. Until this transformation occurs, the mystical door will not open. If it should open prematurely, it would only stir up the person's ambition, tempt him to violate the stability of a normal life and possibly cause him to give up what is important today in exchange for what is important tomorrow. The truth of immortality is the truth of everyday life. Thus, if shallow worldly interest does not die, true evolution of the integral being cannot take place. The keys to the mystical door of divine immortality are given only to those who have transcended all worldly ambition and realized their virtuous fulfillment. These keys have been clearly revealed, but one must go through the different stages of development to understand what the ancient developed ones wrote and taught. An achieved person is one who holds the secret not only of his own life but all of nature. Such a person may roam eternally with and join the unruling rulers and uncreating creators of the multi-universe."

∽ 61 ∽

"Venerable Teacher, if we are worthy enough, would you instruct us how to practice our self-cultivation?"

"Kind prince, long before the beginning of written language, the mystical knowledge of the beginning and development of the universe was directly known by the very ancient developed ones whose minds were at one with the Universal Mind. It was revealed that the developing universe is the expression of its subtle nature which is the same reality as the subtle truth of being and nonbeing and the subtle law of all existence and nonexistence. This development and its law is not the same thing as the duality of lawmakers and followers in the human world. The development of the universe is its own law, its own reason, and its own way as the totality of one life. Therefore, to the narrative mind it is unnamable and beyond description. In other words, by looking at the outer physical universe and its movements one can discover the physical universe and its mechanisms. With developed vision, spiritually developed ones can see the law, the truth, reason, and way of the self-born, self-operating, self-generating, and regenerating essence of the multi-natural world and use simple language to call it Tao. Tao does not exist sometime or somewhere else, but is everywhere and at all times now. From the perception of the developed vision of the whole, the first divisions of manifestation from the Subtle One were called yin and yang, yin being the physical manifestation that is symbolized by a broken line (− −), while manifestation of subtle energy, or yang, is symbolized by an unbroken line (−−). The integration of these two was called Tai Chi (☯).

"A human being is a model of the integration of yin and yang, with physical energy manifesting as the body and subtle energy manifesting as the mind and spirit. Further, the ancients referred to these three aspects of the universe as Heaven (symbolized by three solid lines ☰) which is yang, Earth (symbolized by three broken lines ☷) which is yin, and Man (symbolized by Tai Chi ☯) which is integration of the yin and yang.

"The ancient sages also expressed the development of the universe numerically. The number one represented the Subtle Origin, while two represented the duality of yin and yang, and three the trinity of yin, yang, and their integration as Tai Chi, which brings forth life. These are considered the three main categories of the Universe.

"The number four represents the four basic forces of the universe which are variations of yin and yang: the strong force which was referred to as 'old yang' (⚌); the weak force which was called 'old yin' (⚏); the heavy force which was called 'young yang' (⚎); and the light force which was called 'young yin' ($\equiv\equiv$). For a force to be strong does not necessarily mean that it is heavy, nor is a weak force necessarily light. It is possible for a force to be both light and strong or weak and heavy. These four forces may be considered as parallels to what modern physics terms strong nuclear force ($\equiv$), gravity ($\equiv\equiv$), weak nuclear force ($\equiv\equiv$), and electromagnetism ($\equiv\equiv$). The harmonization of these four forces creates a fifth united force, a Tai Chi, which is the harmonizing force of the universe, a common field. The ancient sages called all five forces the Five Great Performers of the Universe (Wu Hsing), and symbolized them with five physical manifestations. Water symbolized the strong force characterized by aggregation, contraction, collection, and condensation. Fire symbolized the weak force characterized by expansion, disaggregation, dispersion, and dissipation. Wood symbolized the light force characterized by explosion and dynamism. Metal symbolized the heavy force characterized by gravity. The inherent nature of these four different forces battle and conquer each other, while earth symbolizes the united, harmonized, and neutral force among them.

"The Five Great Performers are a very useful system in the practice of internal alchemy. Fire symbolizes mental energy or spirit; water symbolizes sexual energy or general vitality; wood symbolizes male energy; metal symbolizes female energy. Earth harmonizes all incompatible pairs of energy and works as an intermediary between them; it enables the integration of all forces as a Tai

Chi. The Mystical Pass appears to one who has practiced internal alchemy as the Five Performers disintegrate at the culmination of life in the physical realm. The Mystical Pass is the key enabling a breakthrough into the immortal realm. This is the great transformation of a human life from the gross realm of the cycle of life and death to the exquisite realm of absolute freedom and eternal life.

"One can achieve this transformation not through attempting to create a way, but through discovering the way. Human beings cannot create anything on the subtle level outside of their beings. They can give birth to spiritual entities which would become the composite elements of their new life in the spiritual realm. However, through breaking away from the old and connecting with the new, one may spiritually outlive one's physical life. With developed vision one discovers the mystical keys which unlock the secrets of spiritual life in the multi-universe and the universe of natural and orderly progression. To understand the orderly world, the first key is Tai Chi, the ultimate truth of existence; the second is the Great Two, displayed as a parade of yin and yang; the third is the Three Main Categories expressed by Heaven, Earth, and Man; the fourth is the Four Forces, the strong force, the weak force, the light force and the heavy; the fifth is the Five Great Performers of the Universe symbolized by water, fire, wood, metal, and earth; the sixth is the Six Chi or Six Breaths which manifest as Tai Yang (☰), Shao Yang (☳), Yang Ming (☴), Tai Yin (☷), Shao Yin (☵), and Chiu Yin (☶) which express themselves in the transformation of the human organs and as climatic influences of wind, cold, heat, moisture, dryness, and inflammation.

"The seventh key is the process of change and recycling. The eighth is the Eight Great Manifestations,

☰	☷	☵	☲
Heaven	Earth	Water	Fire
☳	☱	☴	☶
Thunder	Lake	Wind	Mountain

with vast categories of each as the Great Transformations of the Universe.

The Eight Great Manifestations generate the sixty-four hexagrams with 384 lines which display all possible combinations of yin and yang. These important systems reveal the truth of Nature and the ways of manifesting all situations and self-transformations of life. There are also many other profound diagrams which help unlock the mystical gate of the subtle evolution of the universe, of human history and of individual lives. Some diagrams will be shown to help illustrate these systems."

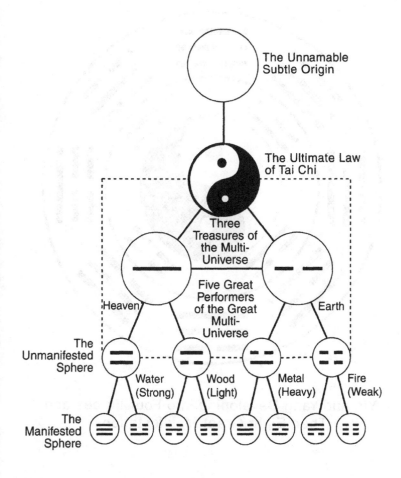

The Unnamable Subtle Origin

The Ultimate Law of Tai Chi

Three Treasures of the Multi-Universe

Five Great Performers of the Great Multi-Universe

Heaven

Earth

The Unmanifested Sphere

Water (Strong)

Wood (Light)

Metal (Heavy)

Fire (Weak)

The Manifested Sphere

From the Subtle Origin to Infinity

Yin and Yang Developing into Four Forces and
Then Eight Great Manifestations

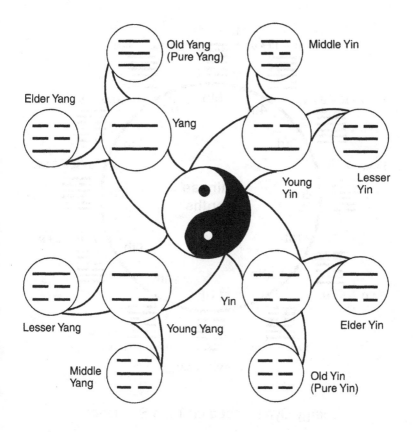

The Center Part of the Sixty-four Dimensions

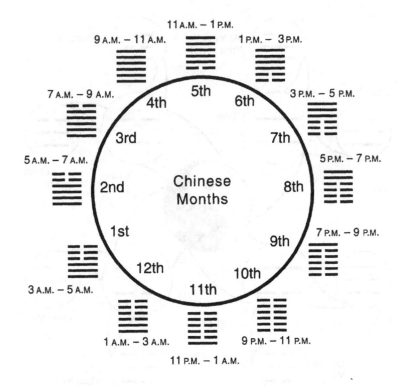

Energy Cycle Based on Time Sequence

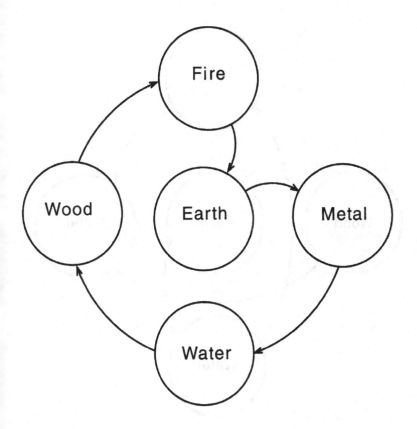

Normal and Regular Cycle of Energy Flow

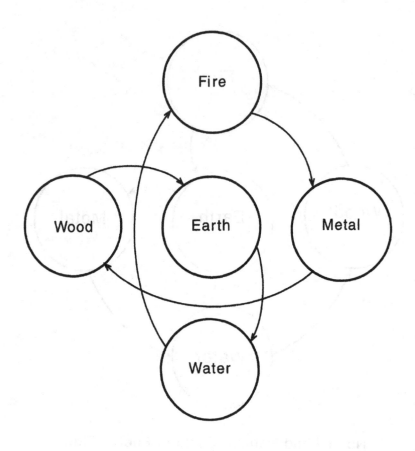

Abnormal Cycle of Energy Flow

~ 62 ~

"Venerable Teacher," asked the wise prince, "may I know something more about the Three Main Categories of the multi-universe?"

"Kind prince, the development of a human being's inner vision corresponds to his spiritual evolution throughout many lifetimes. There are a few individuals who have achieved a complete vision of the multi-universe, especially the whole truth of the Three Main Categories which are the most essential and profound truth of the expansion and exhibition of the vast multi-universe."

"Venerable Teacher, I have discovered that as my inner vision expands its range, the universe seems to expand also. This process is similar to the way in which the traditional healing points were discovered; the points were always there, but with experience generation after generation discovered more and more points and groups of points to use in healing practices."

"Kind prince, your intention to know more about the Three Main Categories is commendable. Truly, the inner vision of the multi-universe was intuitively developed through many generations of people of whole vision, similar, as you say, to the way in which the energy points of the body were discovered. It is important to understand, however, that these truths were merely discoveries and not inventions of the human mind. The human mind is incapable of inventing or creating anything as its own contribution to the divine order of the universe.

"Kind prince, the unfolding of one's inner vision is a natural process which corresponds with the inner growth of the individual. It happens spontaneously. If one tries to formalize discoveries of spiritual truth into rigid doctrines to be taught to others as a means of establishing a train of followers, then one will invariably mislead people and impair their inner growth. If people take these truths for granted, their significance is diminished and they become mere emotional tranquilizers for the undeveloped majority of mankind.

"These discoveries were passed down as a standard of individual development by people whose inner vision had become connected to the entire truth of the universe. I am willing to give you the outline, but I will leave the details of this knowledge to be completed by those who truly cultivate and develop themselves."

"Venerable Teacher, may I know why Heaven is considered one of the Three Treasures?"

"Kind prince, the total reality of the universe is energy; it is called prime energy or prime chi. Two divisions of this energy occur: the heavy, physical energy of the earth and the light, spiritual energy of heaven. The three divisions of this energy are the physical, the spiritual, and a combination of the two.

"Human life represents one whole category of the natural energy flow. The ancient developed ones used the three divisions of energy to distinguish the energy in an individual human being: spiritual energy being centered in the head, physical energy in the belly, and harmonized energy in the heart and mind.

"Spiritual energy is not equally pure at all levels, and each of the Three Main Categories has its own purity: Yu Ching, Shan Ching, and Tai Ching. As we have already seen, these unified energies can be applied to both the macrocosm and the microcosm. To the ancient achieved ones, the purity of the three different levels was the goal of personal achievement. One who achieved himself spiritually attained the range of Yu Ching; one who achieved himself by attaining the wisdom that is connected with universal mindedness or universal heartedness attained the range of Shan Ching; and one who achieved himself by refining his sexual energy attained the range of Tai Ching. The one who achieved himself with all three, expressed in an integral and virtuous life, attained Tao.

"Kind prince, an individual's very being is composed of all the various energies of the universe which are expressed in the different physical characteristics and inherent subtle attributes of human life. These differences are clues to the subtle origin of the energies of the individual and to the origin of nature.

"An individual human being is a small model of the multi-universe, with a hidden and profound nature that is connected to the heavenly realms. Nevertheless, the development of most human beings follows a narrow track which makes them partial and incomplete and thus causes them to lose their appreciation for the great variety that composes the unity of nature."

"Venerable Teacher, I deeply appreciate the completeness of the spiritual achievement of the ancient developed ones, and I admire their complete inner vision."

~· 63 ·~

"Kind prince," said the master, "Heaven is another name for the Three Realms of Purity. It is, therefore, a triad within the triad of the universe. Earth and Man are also parts of the greater triad as well as triads in and of themselves.

"In the Three Main Categories of the multi-universe, the Realm of Great Purity, Tai Ching, is where the productive earth and myriad things reside. It is the lower or outer sphere of nature. The Realm of High Purity, Shan Ching, is where the subtle mind resides; it is the middle sphere. The Realm of Ultimate Purity, Yu Ching, is the residence of the immortal, divine beings, and the most exquisite energy of the universe. All three of these spheres are generated from and rooted in one chi, the Divine Subtle Origin.

"In the achievement of a spiritually developed being, the mode of being in the Realm of Tai Ching is three dimensional and has three components: Hsiang, pure appearance; Chi, natural, healthy, vital energy; and Li, pure law and reason.

"When one reaches the Realm of Shan Ching, the layer of gross, material form is ineffective and the mode of being further harmonizes Hsiang, Chi, and Li. The beings of this realm are still individually distinguishable, however.

"When one reaches Yu Ching, the Realm of Li or pure law, there is no confinement by the distinction of

Chi and no rigidity of material force or form. The beings of this realm have complete freedom, for they are one with pure law. The life of a being in this realm is absolutely straight and direct. If there is any slight crookedness of being, or even a slight deviation or separation from Li, the being is immediately downgraded to the realm of duality and subjected to the control of the two laws of Chi and Li; he is the servant of these two masters. The further the being is downgraded, the more physical law is imposed. The further the downfall of a person, the more forces he is subjected to and bound by in the form of laws. This includes the multiple bondage of material, flesh-centered life.

"At a certain stage the societies of certain tribes of the human race were unlawful. Civilization brings law, but in an evolved society of developed individuals moral law is a matter of common commitment among all people. Once one lifts oneself above all grossness and contamination within one's own being, pure law may manifest itself again. This is the way to become one with pure law.

"Kind prince, within the Three Realms of Great Nature there are numerous small universes. Each of these is called a 'cave universe,' and this physical universe is one of those. To the undeveloped, the universe is an isolated world. Insulated by darkness, the beings who live in one cave universe are unaware of the existence of other cave universes. A highly evolved being, however, can break through the bondage of many layers of darkness.

"Kind prince, nonimpulsiveness is the highest expression of an integral being. All high virtues are accomplished within this pure law, but do you think there are many who are able to follow it? No, kind prince. Worldly people are restless and impulsive, they suffer from their lack of self-control and thus evoke many laws. Highly evolved people have their own conscience as pure law.

"Most people are born with heavy, gross energy and live their lives in bondage to the laws of the material plane. The more restless a person becomes, the stronger the bondage will be. In order to cooperate with pure law, quiescence must be established and maintained. By not touching the gross world and by avoiding any strife they are saved from bondage.

"Kind prince, the truth of the universe is uncovered when one simplifies all aspects of one's life. Simplification is the highest discipline of this sacred tradition. Refinement of one's personality and the channelling of one's refined sexual energy upwards to the higher centers of one's being is the method of true evolution. There are very few people who are able to evolve highly. By breaking through all hindrances step by step, they gradually come to the Realm of High Purity. At first they go up and down with uncertainty and instability until they completely uplift themselves. Then, layer by layer, they evolve to higher and higher planes.

"The integration of yin and yang and the elimination of all mental duality are the real vehicles of immortal life. The Universal Way is simple to understand and easy to follow, yet people wander away from their integral nature

and become lost in ideological and theological mists of
their own creation. Once one knows to stop this wander-
ing and return to simplicity, the Integral Way of the
angels reappears once again. When the lost wanderer returns to his divine origin, integral universal awareness
will bring him great reward."

～· 64 ·～

"Venerable Teacher, would you instruct us in how we
may cultivate ourselves so that we may have contact with
the subtle truth of the multi-universe?"

"Kind prince, people whose intellects are overly developed or who are skeptical about the subtle truth can
effectively restore the wholeness of their minds through
integrating the internal and external elements of their
being. The way to achieve this integration is to learn how
to evoke a specific response from the subtle energy of the
universe. A good and available tool for the public is the
Inquiry of the Changing Signs. By using specific methods,
with an uncalculating mental attitude, an individual can
discover the subtle alternations of yin and yang which
operate within and influence all events of life. In order to
evoke an accurate manifestation from the subtle energy
when inquiring into the changing signs, one must regulate
one's mind, for a regulated mind is the power which manifests an accurate response in physical terms. A clear mind
is the eye of one's being, while a confused mind blinds
one's true eye.

"Every single event that occurs in the universe is a Tai Chi containing both yin and yang, and all individual events combine into one great event which is also a Tai Chi. The alternation of yin and yang is the inevitable truth of the universe. This natural phenomenon is clearly observable in the alternation of day and night; however, in many areas of life the alternation is not so easy to observe. The Inquiry of the Changing Signs is a method which enables one to determine how to be in harmony with the subtle laws of the universe in all activities of life. The changing signs indicate the alternation of yin and yang in specific circumstances; by learning to recognize, classify, understand, and utilize them with the rational mind and also with one's intuition, one may learn to deal with all the circumstances that occur in life. This is only the superficial use of the Inquiry of Changing Signs, however. The highest use of these principles lies in using them to harmonize all the elements of one's being and return to a state of integral oneness.

"Kind prince, the integral beings of the primordial communities of Earth knew no strife, either among themselves or with the rest of the world. In all of their activities they did nothing to violate the subtle alternation of yin and yang, but lived in harmony with their natural and social environment. There was no need, therefore, to develop methods of obtaining foreknowledge. As time passed, however, people began to deviate from their integral nature and it became necessary for them to practice the Inquiry of the Changing Signs, especially when making decisions about important matters such as military action, hunting expeditions, marriage, and so forth. With the information they received from the Inquiry of the Changing Signs they were able to make decisions that were in harmony with natural law and therefore avoid unnecessary trouble and sacrifice.

"Kind prince, in the multi-universe, the high truth known as Tao is the only thing that gives great constancy. Everything else is governed by the great law of transformation. The invariable Tao is the constant nature and Universal Way of the universe, yet within it is contained the variability of the myriad things. Through observing the changes in the myriad things, one may come to recognize the constancy of Tao, for the myriad things are merely variations of the one, original chi. The deep and subtle essence behind all change is constancy. Kind prince, with spiritual cultivation, the awareness of the subtle alternations of yin and yang becomes deeper and deeper. Through searching for the changeless element that exists behind the myriad fluctuations, one may discover the source of all variation, the key to the great transformation. In this way, one uses variation to find the immutable; once the immutable is discovered, one may embrace it.

"By uniting one's being with the constant creative nature of the universe, one may achieve mastery of the great law of transformation in all spheres of life. This is how the Universal Way is discovered and the state of duality transcended. The restless and inquisitive mind will be dissolved and find true peace through complete union with the Tao.

"Kind prince, if the mind of a person who uses the predictive method of Inquiry of the Changing Signs is only partially developed, the benefit he derives will be very limited. To be motivated by the desire to know only whether one will gain or lose something in the material sphere of life is to limit oneself by the bounds of one's own self interest. If these methods become the tool of egotism and selfishness, they could even become dangerous. Yet, if one's mind is fully developed and one uses the subtle knowledge for the purpose of achieving Oneness, one will be nurtured through the understanding of the complete truth.

"Kind prince, when the long age of confusion begins, people will undertake important endeavors, guided only by their own impulses. They will no longer refer to predictive methods for determining whether their actions will be in harmony with the subtle law; this art will be lost to the masses. Yet, even in the confused times of the future, the ancient predictive arts will be a testable way for people to return to the integrity of their own being. By developing the ability to know the future by knowing the subtle pictures formalized in one's own mind, people may rediscover how to live in harmony and how to control the negative tendencies of the mind.

"The great self-examining systems of this ancient tradition guide all young life to study and to reach self-development; this is what it takes to uplift oneself. If the entire system is studied and its principles understood, one will gradually achieve mastery of the whole truth, knowing even the unhappened parts of an event. Every event is the necessary result of external decisive factors and the subtle picture in the subjective mind. It is not hard to recognize the influence that comes about through the harmony or disharmony between the subjective mind and objective fact.

"In general situations, people can exercise their free will to engage in a not-wholly-developed matter. But, if free will is recognized, the responsibility of success and failure belongs to the one who exercises his free will. For the most part, it should be the person himself who forms his mind and his future through cultivating the mind, refining the personality, and adjusting attitudes toward challenging external situations.

"Kind prince, the self-examining systems are only one aspect of the discipline of flexibility of this ancient spiritual art. It is important to remember that a good predictive method is a tool for reaching out beyond the limited realm of the mind. Above this level lies the boundless and profound ocean of spirit which cannot be touched by the mind. The attainment of the highest mental and spiritual levels requires very deep involvement and commitment. Only through total dedication to one's spiritual evolution can one lift oneself to the integral oneness of the Subtle Origin, the Tao."

65

"Venerable Teacher, in all of our discussions it would seem that the human mind is capable of being as familiar with the entire universe as it is with the fingers and palm of one's own hand. It seems as if there is nothing that can escape the observation of the human eye and the penetration of the developed human mind."

"Kind prince," replied the master, "the truth is that the only thing that can be perceived with the senses is the thin shell of reality. The physical universe in which people live is merely the small but important reproductive vision of the divine Mysterious Mother. All of the galaxies, nebulae, stars, planets, and other heavenly bodies exist in the outer wall of the Mysterious Mother's womb. The interplay of yin and yang creates the expansion and contraction of nature and brings forth all things. This interplay of yin and yang, however, expresses the creative universal nature which is behind the movement.

"The whole being of the great goddess is of an unfathomable depth. The Universal Heart is her heart and the Divine Pure Law is her pure being.

"Most of humanity starts and ends in the first stage of life, centered around the reproductive organs, without looking for any further development. Its life activities are still at the stage of being which produces seeds and eggs whose behavior is determined by blind, biological impulse. Such lives are limited to the link with the mystical reproductive valley of the Mysterious Mother, but have not yet reached the center where high reason is activated.

"Union of yin and yang brings forth the manifestation of life, while their disintegration results in the manifestation of death. As life evolves from the lowest level of the one-celled organism to the human level where two genders are clearly distinguishable, the incompleteness of yin and yang energies within an individual becomes more obvious. On the physical level, the very essences of life need to be paired in order to produce a new life. Although a human being appears to be complete and independent, in truth, one's energy is not complete. Individuals need to pair themselves to complete and unite the yin and yang energies within themselves in order to bring forth a new life. When an individual's subtle yin and yang energies are refined and indestructibly integrated, he is born into a higher plane of immortal life.

"Kind prince, people become bewildered by the myriad manifestations of the physical sphere of the universe. They dissect the world into small parts and perceive only fragments of the physical environment. They see only the bushes and not the forest. All exploration and adventure in the ordinary sense never go beyond the reproductive sphere of the universe; the divine being of the Mysterious Mother is never reached by most people. Only those who are very highly evolved have the opportunity to break through all obstructions and reach the universal-heartedness and pure reason of the Mysterious Mother."

66

"Kind prince, all life is brought forth as a result of the integration of yin and yang. When a seed and an egg unite within a female, a new life is conceived. This is the first integration of yin and yang in the human sphere. The second integration of yin and yang takes place when the physically mature male and female interrelate sexually. This union may bring about the integration of yin and yang, but it may not bring about the integration of the egg and the seed of each partner. It may appear to ordinary eyes that the birth of a human being is the beginning of a new life, but a human life at this stage of development has not yet been born into the spiritual light which is characterized by complete understanding and high wisdom. Unless an individual is born into the immortal realm, a third integration of yin and yang cannot happen.

"Life in the physical sphere is a preparation for birth into the subtle realm. Everything born into the physical world must die; however, a developed individual who learns the Immortal Way may be born again into a life of absolute freedom. A subtle transformation takes place within an individual when he succeeds in cultivating himself and attains pure wisdom. Immortal cultivation is a gradual process of practicing pure diet, energy conducting exercises (Tow Ying), and the cultivation and refinement of one's whole being (Shu Liang). With this the heavy, gross energy of one's life begins to diminish. All of these practices are the preparation for breaking through the cycle of birth, procreation, and death, and emerging into the immortal divine one.

"As an individual's energy becomes more refined and subtle, he comes under the dominant control of the physical realm less and less. As such a life evolves, it gradually becomes submerged in the mighty ocean of spiritual energy, the Universal Divine Energy, and a new life, governed by wisdom rather than emotion, is thus created. As one's sense of life broadens, the psychological ego is dissolved and the entire body is positively influenced. As one subtly transforms oneself, one leaves the gross realm and approaches immortal divinity. The evolution of the soul depends on the growth of self-awareness. This takes place over the course of many lifetimes through learning the Universal Way and following the precise and explicit methods of self-cultivation which are the heritage of the accomplished angels. The third integration of yin and yang is the mystical conception of a new immortal life.

"Kind prince, life which is born of flesh and blood must inevitably die. Life which is born by cultivating the integration of the subtle energies of yin and yang never dies. Although every human life begins with the integration of yin and yang, life produces continual self-splitting in a geometric progression, expressed by the I Ching as pure whole energy splitting itself into —— and —— . There is then further endless progression and finally complete distintegration. The possibility of achieving immortal life lies in restoring the integration of yin and yang and becoming whole once again. Immortality comes with the practice of virtue that embraces the essence of all life."

~· 67 ·~

"Venerable Teacher, it is my firm and immutable decision to follow the Universal Way as the only guidance in my life and to practice the integration of yin and yang as my self-cultivation so that my life will be a complete model of Tai Chi.

"The way to integrate my own yin and yang is to discard all lofty and fanciful thinking and argumentative discussion and to follow the invariable principles of the integral truth. If I must practice cultivation by myself, I will steadily move through all the phases of spiritual evolution step by step. The individual practice of self-cultivation is the foundation of all high spiritual achievement, just as you have taught us. Nature supplies me with physical vitality, just as she supplies it to all life at the biological level. I will sublimate my sexual energy so that it becomes wisdom and then transform my wisdom into immortal spirit.

"If blessing is afforded to me, if Heaven allows me, and if my virtue sufficiently supports me, I shall be instructed in the practice of final individual self-integration. If it is suitable to practice dual cultivation, I may experience the direct integration of Tai Chi through the intersection of doubled yin and yang. If my virtue does not support me, if my blessing limits me and if I do not bring any virtuous merit to the world through serving others, I still will be a person of natural integration without doing any harm to my life, if that is possible. Sometime I hope to receive the secret of dual cultivation, for without correct guidance it would only be an abuse that would cause my downfall and ruin my opportunity to achieve immortality rather than fulfill its positive purpose."

The master replied, "Kind prince, the practice of dual cultivation has many different purposes and levels. One is to balance one's energy, for when one's energy is balanced, one's health improves, one's emotions are harmonious, and one's personality becomes smooth and even. Although this certainly has a positive value, its benefit is on a general level. Dual cultivation can be a mental and spiritual discipline, which leads to the achievement of desirelessness. If a person exposes himself to that which is desirable, can he find out if he has transcended desire and refined his impulses?

"At the highest level of dual cultivation, however, one faces differences in energy in order to integrate what one already has within and to bring about a transcendent integration of one's own energy. The form of intercourse is not even necessary in order to achieve immortality.

"The opportunity and the secret to achieving immortality is a reward for someone who has achieved truly great virtue. In the long history of this tradition, such things are taught by the divine immortals to the follower who is able to learn the precious secret of achieving total integration. Even though a person may be boundlessly virtuous, he must also harmonize his life being. Although every human being is an integration of yin and yang, further uniting of yin and yang is necessary for the conception of a higher life. High beings need to continually combine new spheres of yin and yang in order to achieve still higher spheres of life. Thus an individual may need to practice dual cultivation so that he may complete his energy. In the secret method of harmonization of yin and yang, the great sun is the male energy for all female Taoists, while the male Taoists also utilize solar energy to assist their weakened male energy. It does not mean one should live like an animal, just that one must have sufficient yang energy. The earth and the moon are abundant sources of female energy that male Taoists can utilize to support their balance and achieve long, healthy lives. There are some further details for guiding one's energy cultivation. For example, lakes symbolize young female energy, hills symbolize young male energy, etc. These are the potent knowledge and techniques of historical Taoists. The highest qualification of the practitioner in the union of male and female is something I consider a secret of secondary importance, because not many people are able to utilize it. For those of truly great virtue who do not have the opportunity to learn the secret of dual cultivation, the Universal Divine Energy will provide the remedy to support, supplement and complete their energy."

‿ 68 ‿

"Venerable Teacher, may I ask what are the primary principles of angelic dual cultivation?"

"Kind prince, listen well. The primary principles of angelic dual cultivation are contained in these lines which were revealed to me by the immortal beings:

One of integral virtue follows Tao and Tao alone.
Tao, as the Universal Way of the universe, is elusive
    and evasive;
It unveils itself as images and forms.
Evasive and elusive, it discloses itself as indefinable
    substance.
Shadowy and indistinct, it further reveals itself as
    impalpable subtle essence which is so subtle, yet so
    real.
With unfailing sincerity one may know and rejoin this
    subtle reality.
Returning to itself is how the eternal Tao exercises
    itself.
Being gentle and yielding is how the Tao employs
    itself.
All things come from the Manifest, and the Manifest
    comes from the Unmanifest.
The softest of all things can overcome the hardest of
    all things.
Only the insubstantial can penetrate the spaceless.
Thus I know the benefit of nonaction and silence.
There are few under Heaven who can attain it.

"Kind prince, those are the primary principles of angelic dual cultivation. Learn them well, meditate on them, and apply them carefully with correct understanding throughout the interplay of yin and yang in your single or dual cultivation."

◡· 69 ·◠

"Kind teacher," said the prince, "to most people, sexuality is one of the main activities of life. I would like to know some of the Taoist sexual guidance that can help those who wish to lift themselves from the lower level of animal impulse to the higher level of energy integration."

"Kind prince," said the master, "an individual's approach to sexuality is an indication of his level of evolution. There is a vast difference between ordinary human sexual activity and the dual cultivation of a Taoist. In ordinary intercourse, the sexual organs take primary importance while the other organs and systems of the body are subordinate. In this way, the servant controls the master, and one's energy dissipates and becomes disordered.

"Every cell of an individual's being seeks the union of yin and yang, not merely the sexual organs. The purpose of angelic intercourse is the union and completion of an individual's yin and yang energy. It is a process of refinement and sublimation of energy. Once the energy is refined, it is directed upward to the higher centers of one's being. In angelic intercourse, spirit unites with spirit, mind with mind, and every cell of one body with every cell of the other body. It is the spirit, not the sexual organs, which directs such intercourse.

"Another difference is that ordinary intercourse seeks a substantial manifestation as its culmination, while angelic intercourse seeks the intangible union of yin and yang. Angelic intercourse is not completed by a substantial discharge, but rather with the integration of each partner's subtle energy. In this way, angelic intercourse leads to immortality.

"Ordinary intercourse requires making an effort, but in angelic intercourse the love union is achieved spontaneously through nonaction. When one remains very calm and relaxed, the gross sexual impulse diminishes and the subtle energy becomes more developed. The great, subtle transformation takes place naturally and in silence. The whole universe is developed in this way. It happens naturally, not through making it happen.

"In preparation for this sacred instruction, every disciple must extend his virtue to the world in order to accomplish the mission of world peace and purification. One should learn the immortal truth of life. If one extends one's virtue selflessly to the world, the immortal truth will unite with one naturally. The general principles of achieving energy integration have been shown, but the details are usually taught directly by a teacher who has truly achieved himself. By following the right channel of life and by radiating a virtuous influence to the world, one may develop one's subtle energy. In this way one can reconnect oneself with the subtle realms, and the immortals will give their guidance even without a teacher."

"Kind prince, dual cultivation is a key which can enable individuals in the physical realm to realize true liberation. In general, the life of a human being is a complex net woven out of the threads of passion and desire. A person thinks that every single thread is necessary, never realizing the slow, inexorable process of enslavement that is being woven about him. Through reflective self-awareness, one can unravel this self-woven net and free himself from the servitude into which his passionate actions and desires have led him. Once freed of the lower traps of yin and yang duality, one may live naturally, work virtuously without succumbing to egotism, and regain eternal vitality. Through strict regulation of one's activities and creativity, one may become reconnected with the realm of being which enriches one with great potency and in which there are no obstructions. If a person succeeds in this reconnection, he ceases to be a slave and achieves full independence and spiritual autonomy. Kind prince, freedom is not a gift that is given to the individual; it is a task of self-transformation and subjective evolution.

"An individual has the possibility of vanquishing death and rising to the highest realms of being through attracting yang energy from the source of universal life. In order to accomplish this, he must dissolve his yin energy into the luminous substance from which his subtle essence has descended. In this realm of being he is permanently out of danger of relapsing into the cycle of rebirth.

In this realm it is no longer important to have the sense of an individual soul or spirit as the substance of one's life, for one's life is pure nature itself, the constancy of the universe.

"Kind prince, it is essential to understand that an individual must remain one with the constant virtue of life and dissolve the stiffness and rigidity gathered by worldly confrontation. When the internal metamorphosis is complete, he may emerge into a new realm of being in which he is one with Tao. This is the culmination of his evolution into the realm of pure freedom."

‿· 71 ·‿

"Venerable Teacher, all of your disciples are fortunate to have the rare opportunity of receiving this precious instruction directly from you. Many generations from now, during the time of confusion, will people have the opportunity to learn the verbal and nonverbal teachings of this sacred tradition?"

"Kind prince, only after people refine their heavy, gross energy and reach the subtle level can they attain self-mastery. Only after they have attained self-mastery can the principles of self-integration through single or dual cultivation and the unworded teaching be passed on to them. Only then will they be able to derive the benefit of them.

"During the process of purifying the body, mind, and spirit, the gradual transformation toward eternal life occurs. If a teacher instructs a person who has not yet achieved purification and self-mastery, the energy of desire will cause trouble and conflict. Therefore, the careless, general dissemination of this teaching of pure being is not encouraged."

The prince said, "Venerable Teacher, I understand that one who has the opportunity to learn self-cultivation and dual cultivation should maintain right practice in order to achieve spiritual freedom and transcend the dualistic trap of life."

"Kind prince, the tempting angelic dual cultivation is not an exclusive practice. For the purpose of energy balance, sometimes it is a remedy to a weakened male if correctly guided, however all practices and disciplines should be parallel practices; one assists the other. Just as a balance between eating, drinking, and fasting enables one to maintain health, celibacy and dual cultivation work together to enable one to attain internal and external harmony. For reasons of different energy formation in each individual, however, celibacy may be more appropriate than dual cultivation for some people, while for others periodic celibacy is very uplifting. When and how to use these methods may be determined through the guidance of a developed teacher. The highest principle to be followed in spiritual practice is that of energy response; the safest and most effective method is not safe and effective if the natural energy does not harmoniously respond. One's achievement must come from connecting oneself with the Universal Divine Energy; teachers and techniques are but transitional."

"Venerable Teacher, I am very eager to learn the way to enter the divine realm with great spiritual power, and I am willing to undergo the most stringent purification to become worthy of receiving this sacred and precious teaching."

"Kind prince, any merit attained must have come about through extending one's virtue to the world, and any spiritual achievement attained must have been through self-cultivation and union with the original Oneness. This means not engaging in schemes which would separate one from the Universal Way and not forming impulsive ambitions that would cause the loss of wholeness of the mind. The pure mind is an exquisite energy in human life. It is an important part of one's life being with which to cultivate and achieve divine immortality through the virtuous power of kindness, tolerance, and patience. In order to be correct, one's self-cultivation must have as its purpose the integration of one's being with the universal virtuous energy which is the true and durable spiritual energy of the universe. People with a high capability can achieve higher spiritually by doing some ordinary daily work such as healing, but not through imaginary magic for the purpose of satisfying their undeveloped emotions. To compose all virtues into one reality entails developing and extending the virtue one already has; there is no virtue that is not already contained within one's own nature.

"To embrace the integral Oneness, one must not let circumstances of any kind seize one's mind, nor should one let one's mind become so preoccupied that one loses all awareness of present circumstances. On the Universal Way, there is neither mind nor circumstances. There is nothing, and there is no attachment to the nothingness. This is the way to manage one's mind in daily life, whether practicing single or dual cultivation. Only through the elimination of all strife can integral Oneness be attained."

"Venerable Teacher," asked the prince, "is angelic dual cultivation virtuous?"

"Kind prince, angelic dual cultivation is virtuous if practiced correctly and unvirtuous if practiced incorrectly. It is an opportunity for a man and woman to uplift each other spiritually and enjoy the bliss of wholeness."

"Venerable Teacher," asked the prince again, "is marriage suitable for all spiritual people?"

"Kind prince, the marriage system is a social structure which came about in later generations of human development. It should be duly respected, but dual cultivation relies on mutual energy response through divine guidance. It is not motivated by sexual impulse or by the need for financial cooperation in life, but only by spiritual purposes."

~ 73 ~

"Venerable Teacher, should a disciple offer his or her energy to the master in dual cultivation?"

"Kind prince, all teachers and their disciples should offer their talent, wealth, and life to the world. The teacher is the one who offers himself or herself to the disciples. The disciples are his or her world. Between the teacher and disciples is an interplay of spiritual dedication in which the one who is offering cannot be distinguished from the one who is receiving. It is not even possible to distinguish who is the teacher and who is the student. Achieved minds are simply mirrors reflecting one another. The pure energy of a student may be offered to the angels who dwell within the master. Those whose energy is depleted should offer fresh flowers, young plants, newly opened wine and freshly made food, as well as their service, to symbolize and express their spiritual offering. Those who make offerings to the master without self-restraint are blessed with the actualization of breaking away from their physical individuality to live inside of each other. This joy can only happen among selfless beings with pure spiritual devotion. Any small suspicions or jealousy would destroy the great happiness of harmony. Only when their spiritual contamination is cleansed by the students' own efforts, their unhappiness dispersed, will a life of innocent happiness be experienced by good disciples to whom the master offers his heart and achieved knowledge."

∼· 74 ·∼

"Venerable Teacher, in the practices of Taoist cultivation, what deities and divine beings should one connect oneself with for the purpose of energy response?"

"Kind prince," replied the master, "the universe is the body of the godhead. Most of the time we treat it as the great goddess of the feminine principle. The pure being of man and woman are the spiritual symbol as well as the reality of the angelic beings. The Tai Chi circle is the spiritual emblem, and Huh-tu and Lo-shu the divine diagram. The Eight Great Manifestations and sixty-four hexagrams of the I Ching are the revelation of the truth of universal harmony. The sun of fire and the moon of water are the spiritual symbols of masculine and feminine. Mountains are the symbols of the young male, and lakes the symbols of young females. Towers and ponds are built for the spiritual purpose of symbolizing male and female energy and for expressing and evoking specific energy responses from the mystical source. The entire practice is associated with the manifestation of the unimaginable, indescribable Universal Divine Energy. It is beyond the scope of words!"

∼· 75 ·∼

The master continued the dialogue, saying, "Kind prince, look at the silkworm. At first it is only a small pink spot of an egg, but when the spring warmth hatches it, the tiny worm starts to break through its shell and becomes a black grub that feeds on young, green mulberry leaves. As it grows, the black color slowly fades away and the worm becomes fat and white. When it is old enough, it stops eating and begins spitting out silk on all sides of its body to make a cocoon in order to prepare for its second transformation into a pupa. When it emerges from the cocoon as a moth, it has a distinct gender and it copulates with a moth of the opposite sex. After giving his physical essence to the female moth, the male moth dies away. The female moth conceives and brings forth eggs, but then she too dies away. This is the cycle of a silkworm's life, governed entirely by biological law.

"Kind prince, what do you think? From a biological point of view, how much difference is there between a human life and the life of a silkworm?"

"Venerable Teacher, through numberless years of struggling, mankind has grown in self-awareness, yet from the beginning of life, I do not see any difference between silkworms and human beings, except for those individuals who are born of Heaven."

"Kind prince, even those who are Heaven-born must obey the law of human life when they take human form. The law of human beings is basically the same as the law of silkworms."

"Venerable Teacher, I feel sad that even though people develop and grow in self-awareness, they are still bound by the biological pattern of birth, growth, procreation, and death. Is it not a pity that people do not have the opportunity to learn the path of liberation from physical bondage?"

"Kind prince, liberation from physical bondage and high spiritual freedom are not beautiful pavilions in the air. They require a process of continual transformation and evolution with the biological aspect of a human being as its foundation. It involves breaking through the cycle of life and death. It forms the hope of every individual who would attain the freedom of life. Most people's awareness is limited to the short span of their own lifetime and the superficial sphere of their daily life, as they stubbornly insist that these ordinary cycles are the final truth of life. They superstitiously cling to the hope that they will receive salvation through their religious beliefs, thus they see no need to learn the Universal Way of cultivation."

"Venerable Teacher, in future generations and in the time of confusion, will there be good men and women who have the opportunity to know the truth of a free immortal life and who will succeed in breaking through their own cycles of life and death?"

"Kind prince, in future generations, because people procreate as prolifically as the silkworm produces eggs, with little moral control or astrological awareness, there will inevitably be many disabled and sick individuals. This blind and ignorant multiplication of the population will degrade the quality of humanity. In the future there will also be collective murder, slaughter, plagues, and finally a big war with the crisis of total destruction. Because of the destructive tendency of the undeveloped world, this is what seems to be approaching."

"Venerable Teacher, what can we do for the future generations of our descendants?"

"Kind prince, the Universal Way and the eternal truth of life depend on the development of individual self-awareness, not shallow social movements for the multitudes. What is needed is the total awakening of all, so that the majority of people will know to eliminate negative influences in their lives and do what would benefit other people. Integral cultivation is individually based because it involves personal self-transformation and breaking through the individual's cycle of insatiability. Each individual is responsible for his own evolution, but true achievement comes mostly from one's virtuous fulfillment in helping and serving his fellow man.

"The teaching service is to show the way to those of great potential virtue. Surely, the teacher gives a strong positive discipline for self-cultivation, however, he cannot perform an individual's self-cultivation for him nor undergo the disciple's self-transformation. If there is no teacher, there is no way to receive the training and discipline necessary for continual cultivation. The teacher is a subtle mold in which the disciple may shape himself. If the disciple can maintain enough malleability to transform himself inwardly and outwardly, he may derive a new spirit and a new life. There is a saying that only by breaking down his resistance to the new can a disciple receive the new light.

"A teacher of integral life is an angel who resides in the world to help people. He radiates his virtue to nourish his surroundings and, if he is misunderstood by people, he does not stop extending his virtue to them. Also with his integral awareness, he cannot be enslaved by the world. In future generations the world may not become a slaughterhouse, if teachers of integral life are respected and their precious teaching seen as the safeguard of each generation of life."

"Venerable Teacher, I wish for all divine beings to have mercy on humankind and save them from perishing."

"Kind prince, a time of world destruction will not come in the future in which many lives are lost if those who are able to save themselves and the world practice selfless virtuous fulfillment and follow the Universal Way of life. Only the ones of immortal virtue will be able to support the world and start a better one.

"Human beings are descendants of divine origin, but they have degraded themselves generation after generation until, at last, all self-awareness has been lost. In their blindness, they could easily destroy themselves and the world they live in. In the human world this has happened on a small scale many times before, particularly at the climax of some human cultures. But a new world has always been re-created by virtuous beings. These events have been known to the highly developed ones for a long time. Kind prince, virtuous people are concerned with the future of all lives. Beside the positive, virtuous efforts to awaken their fellow man to trust in the divine subtle law which manifests in Tai Chi, there is always the remedy of the extreme offsetting itself by overexpansion."

⁓· 76 ·⁓

The master continued, "Kind prince, all who follow the guidance in this scripture will attain the correct awareness of the integral, universal life of truth. Their minds will become calm and they will develop subtle potency. They will extend their virtue unconditionally to all of their fellow beings. When integral virtue prevails in the world, neither the potencies of the spirits of physical nature nor the rulers of the world can do any harm. When the potencies of the spirits of physical nature and the rulers of the world merge into one united whole, all virtuous energy will unite and benefit all life."

"Venerable Teacher," said the prince, "allow me to make my vow before my only teacher, the one of universal, integral virtue. I vow to embrace the integral Oneness and ignore all divergence. As an expression of the divine nature of my life, I vow to extend integral, universal virtue to the world without making personal consideration first in importance."

"Kind prince, one who realizes his virtuous responsibility to quietly offer himself to others without expecting a reward or honor can be entrusted with the life of the entire world. Indeed, he becomes the savior of the world."

"Venerable Teacher, should this scripture be called The Thorough Emancipation of the Mind, although in truth there is no mind to emancipate, or should it be called the Integration of Universal Mind? Will the general public in the future time of confusion be able to benefit from such high instruction? Will it even be powerful enough to lead sensitive individuals out of darkness?"

"Kind prince," asked the master, "Will the people of the future be less intelligent?"

"Venerable Teacher," replied the prince, "I think people of the future will be more intelligent, so I do not understand why there will be more trouble in the future. Although life will be more abundant, people will be more unhappy. Why is this so?"

"Wise prince," replied the master, "it will be from the misuse and partial development of intelligence that a time of confusion will arise and grow progressively worse. People will lose their appreciation for a healthy natural life of plainness after being attracted to and entrapped by all kinds of accumulated bad habits. Slavery will pervade human life and all human relationships under different names and reasons. If one is not the slave of social undevelopment, he will be the slave of all kinds of emotional entrapment; if not the slave of his desires, then the slave of his ego. The forms of slavery are many. Most people become slaves to natural demands, fashionable luxuries, social power, artificial religion or ideology, destiny, and most of all, psychological excuses. All kinds of unnecessary conflict will be brought about, aggravating turmoil and creating unprecedented calamity on a large scale.

"Kind prince, the Universal Way will be available at all times and places for the problems of individuals and the world. There will be great people who awaken during the era of great confusion and darkness. Through a vast social renaissance, the awakening of the universal divine nature within people will be reached. Its true foundation rests on the people who will achieve themselves through individual emancipation and self-cultivation.

"To achieved individuals, it is true that there is no mind to be emancipated, and neither is there any mind to be enslaved, but, in general, people create a variety of complicated situations and become stuck in their concepts and false images. They remain unaware of the situation on the large scale by being stuck and trying to convince others to follow what they think is right. Thus, confusion is added to confusion and slaves follow other slaves in a terrible darkness.

"Kind prince, what do you think? Will a person become very different as an individual after being emancipated from all kinds of slavery?"

"Venerable Teacher, before being emancipated from all kinds of slavery, one lives like a blind man who continually falls into the mud and does not complain of his blindness, but only of being in the mud. One who has emancipated himself from slavery of all kinds sees the light at all times."

"Kind prince, to an integrally achieved one, there is no more blindness and no more mud, so there is no more separation of any kind. Complete emancipation takes place only when one integrates all aspects of a natural, healthy life.

"The Integral One dissolves all shallow, sensory discrimination in order to serve the Universal Oneness of integral life. The Integral One does not even strive to embrace Oneness, because to do so would establish the concepts of self and Oneness. Oneness is all embracing, and it is also non-embracing. The Integral One embraces nothing, because there is nothing to hinder him from extending his true nature to embrace all things and beings. The Integral One is simply natural and truthful. To be nothing apart from one's true nature is to be all."

"Venerable Teacher, will people become so afraid of being enslaved that they will not dare to do anything at all?"

"Kind prince, a person of complete emancipation has also emancipated himself from the concept of being a slave. People who look for true mastery should realize that mastery comes from lowering oneself. They should not be afraid of being positively committed to living a virtuous life. Those who restore their true nature achieve balance, integration, and harmony. They become universal beings whose virtue is complete and impartial.

"When one is completely emancipated from what he has built around himself, what is left is his pure nature. A person can then spontaneously release his pure energy in daily life, so that his very essence is connected with the entire universe. He is thus regarded as a person of truth.

"A person of truth is a living divinity. He is not only above his mind, but he can be above the laws of physical nature. He actually becomes one with all. When he moves, the universe moves. When he sleeps, the universe sleeps. This is not merely a philosophical notion; it is living truth. A person of truth is so simple that he cannot be distinguished from other people, yet he can be recognized by those who have developed to the same level."

⌁ 78 ⌁

"Venerable Teacher," said the prince, "you have shown us the way to integralness so that those who aspire to learn it in the future will clearly be able to understand that the Universal Way is a matter of living wholly and not the religious invention of a desperate mind. It is pure universal mind itself, not a mental concept. It is the depth of the wholesome mind, not mere cleverness that reacts to external circumstance. It is pure energy, not the mirage which people mistake for spiritual achievement. It is the continuous development of life with its spirits, not the result of hypnosis. It is the plain, natural truth, not philosophical fantasy. It is invariable, universal law, not a cultural flower produced by one time and place. It is the eternal unfolding of life, not a psychological approach to quiet the troubled, wounded mind. It is total reality, not an occult practice. It is the true way of fulfillment in life.

"The Universal Way is the constant, immutable truth of the multi-universe. Any oddity, strangeness, or fanaticism goes against it. Extravagant lifestyles, fancy food, and raucous music spoil the serenity of the mind and dull one's subtlety; life becomes barren and one's spiritual unfolding is obstructed. The Universal Way values simplicity, plainness, and virtue in speech, dress, and behavior far more than that which is exciting, dazzling, and fashionable. Through establishing honesty in every facet of life, one may return to the simple essence of life. Excessiveness and extremes are contrary to the Universal Way and are therefore never practiced by one who follows the Way of wholeness.

"Venerable Teacher, I truly understand that the development of one's being through self-cultivation is the only correct way of life. Because a human being is so malleable, whatever one cultivates is what one becomes. If one tries to practice cultivation by following a particular religious doctrine, one becomes a slave to partiality. Worldly religion is meant to hold some people of the world, but it also creates disharmony among people on a larger scale. When one takes a single step outside the human sphere of life, all religious practices become useless because they are nothing more than hypnotic, psychological techniques for manipulating an undeveloped mind. The habitual effect of religion on the mind is a real obstacle to pure spiritual growth, and when one departs from artificial teachings and is free of any religious control, one may find that no spiritual evolution has taken place by merely following a religion. Is it not a pity that so many are manipulated by the misbelief that religion can save their souls?"

"Kind prince, if one's spiritual pursuit is partial, one's development is partial. Integral beings are completely evolved from and in the human sphere, having refined the three spheres of energy of a human being. When one cultivates oneself correctly, an internal transformation takes place. The internal metamorphosis is subtle and gradual, and is usually unobservable to those who are undeveloped. When one's energy is ripe, however, the old self is transformed just as a caterpillar is transformed into a beautiful butterfly.

"Kind prince, if one does not find the right way of refining one's physical energy to become spiritual immortal elixir, and merely looks for philosophical or psychological satisfaction, he will not be able to break through his human, biological limitations and evolve to a higher state of being.

"Before a person achieves transformation from the gross sphere to the subtle spiritual realms, he may return to the dusty world many times. His life experiences may be similar or different each time, but the general rule is that if a person takes the partial events of his life either too seriously or too lightly, he spoils his opportunity.

"Once a person achieves complete transformation and sublimation, he becomes unfathomable. No ordinary means of measuring or judging can be applied to him. He is an Integral One who can come and go as anyone else, but his essence of life always exists. He can do and make good things happen but not necessarily through himself. There is nothing that he is unable to do. He extends his pure life to many bodies which appear in different places and can do many things at the same time, because, in truth, he has attained the subtle, cosmic body. He is the one who can actualize all positive virtues but keeps to the subtle source. This is not a mere philosophical notion. One will miss the truth of an Integral Being by not realizing true self-cultivation.

"An integral being can outlive any time and any generation. Mere understanding does not enable one to become an integral being, but through actual self-cultivation and direct realization, one verifies the truth and fulfills the integral truth by being it. The truth is here in the simple essence of life when one is ready to accept it, but people look for it instead in faraway shadows."

⌣ 79 ⌣

"Venerable Teacher, in the future time of confusion, will the one who studies and practices this scripture be able to gain the integral vision of Tao?"

"Kind prince, the one who studies and practices this scripture will attain the insight to see through to the integral truth."

"Venerable Teacher, will those of the future who study and practice this scripture acquire the subtle light of wisdom?"

"Kind prince, they will acquire the subtle light that illuminates all time and space."

"Venerable Teacher, will those who study and practice this scripture in the future acquire the mightiest sword of superior mind?"

"Kind prince, those who study and practice this scripture will obtain the sharp sword of clarity that thrusts through all entanglements and obstruction."

"Venerable Teacher, will those who study and practice this scripture in the future obtain the mystical pearl of full development?"

"Kind prince, they will grow a mystical pearl of full development which can expand to envelop the entire universe and can also gather itself into an invisible seed of smallness."

"Venerable Teacher, will those who study and practice this scripture in the future achieve the undaunted moral courage and undestroyable power of Integral Nature?"

"Kind prince, they shall achieve the undaunted moral courage and undestroyable power of Integral Nature.

"What do you think, kind prince: can one describe the integral vision of Tao?"

"No, Venerable Teacher, the integral vision of Tao cannot be described. However, one could say that when the opening of a fountain is blocked with sand, the fountain cannot flow."

"Kind prince, what is the sand that blocks the vision of the fountain?"

"Venerable Teacher, it is irrational, dualistic vision which blocks the fountain of universal mindedness."

"Kind prince, does the subtle light of wisdom have a specific shape?"

"Venerable Teacher, the subtle light of wisdom is without shape."

"Kind prince, does the mighty sword of clarity have a specific form?"

"No, Venerable Teacher, the mighty sword of clarity is without any form."

"Kind prince, what does the mystical pearl of full development look like?"

"Venerable Teacher, it looks like nothing."

"Kind prince, what do you think? Can the undestroyable Integral Nature be measured?"

"No, Venerable Teacher, the undestroyable Integral Nature is immeasurable. It is absolutely powerful, however."

"Kind prince, those who study and practice the truth of this scripture in future generations will be blessed. By following its integral guidance with sincerity they will gain the most mysterious power. They will become indestructible and will rise above all difficulty and calamity.

"Kind prince, what do you think? Did I obtain any secret knowledge from my master?"

"Venerable Teacher, I truly believe that you received boundless treasures from past masters."

"Kind prince, do you now have the integral vision of Tao?"

"Yes, Venerable Teacher, I have attained the integral vision of Tao through your precious guidance."

"Kind prince, do you now have the mighty sword of wisdom and clarity of superior mind?"

"Yes, Venerable Teacher, I have acquired both through your precious training."

"Kind prince, have you restored the integral nature of indestructibility?"

"Yes, Venerable Teacher, I have restored the integral nature of indestructibility through practicing universal mindedness and universal heartedness."

"Kind prince, are these treasures visible?"

"Venerable Teacher, they are invisible."

"Kind prince, can one assign a name to the all-encompassing integralness?"

"No, Venerable Teacher, although it is referred to as Tao, the integralness of universal beingness is unnamable."

"Kind prince, does Tao exist as something apart from one's own being?"

"No, Venerable Teacher, Tao is not something separate or external to one's own being. However, some human beings who are partially developed spiritually or intellectually will perceive it as such."

"Kind prince, what then is the Tao?"

"Venerable Teacher, I cannot respond in words, I can only embrace it in wholeness."

"Kind prince, do not embrace the Tao. Be the Tao."

~· 80 ·~

"Venerable Teacher, should one live in seclusion and cultivate oneself in order to transcend all worldly troubles and pain or should one courageously take on the troubles and pain of worldly experiences as important elements in attaining enlightenment and integral virtue?"

"Kind prince, if one does not become thoroughly enlightened in order to reach unshakable integralness, one can face neither the solitude of seclusion nor the pressures of living in the world. Only those who are fully enlightened are able to use one hand to assist the other. Enlightenment is the means, virtue is the end. One who is truly wise is virtuous.

"Kind prince, it is not a question of whether one should live in seclusion or in the world. The question is: Will one really achieve complete enlightenment and spiritual freedom, or will one become only partially enlightened? If one achieves only partial enlightenment, he may become clever, sharp-tongued, and so overly sensitive that he is unable to bear the task of living in the practical world. He may insist on isolating himself to enjoy his so-called spiritual pleasures alone, or he may rush to impart his own teachings to the world. In any of these instances, the person deviates from the Tao."

"Venerable Teacher, if all of these alternatives are but a deviation, what is the correct course to take?"

"Kind prince, a great vessel takes a long time to build. An individual's enlightenment is arrived at through long and tedious cultivation. One who desires to reach the climax of his cultivation too soon and strives to publicize himself prematurely may become a false model of virtue and sacrifice the truth or even his own life through ignorance. He may lose himself and mislead others without ever having a chance to correct his wrongdoing if he were to die young. In the future the streets will be full of self-proclaimed, but half-enlightened, teachers who will bring about much confusion."

"Venerable Teacher, the human world seems like a big ship in need of someone to steer it. If there is no one at the helm, it could drift aimlessly into dangerous waters and imperil the lives of all its passengers. There must be someone who is willing to shoulder the responsibility of navigating the vessel of the world. In the future time of confusion, will there be people who are virtuous enough to keep the world headed in a positive direction on its voyage?"

"Kind prince, a person of Tao is not ambitious to be a leader unless the responsibility falls to him; he will make no scheme to take it. He fulfills the task that is assigned to him and then takes no credit and holds no attachment to it. He merely offers to serve others. He knows that individuals are the foundation of human society, thus the way to guide the world is to correctly guide each person who comes to him. This work does not merely skim the surface of the social problem, but goes deeply into the source. Whoever undertakes such an endeavor must prepare himself to meet the following qualifications.

"One must deeply plant and firmly root one's spirit in Tao. One must be truly virtuous and sincere. At a practical level one must be willing to improve himself by eliminating all negative attitudes and habits. In this way one is able to build a stable, broad, receptive, and creative personality. Only then may one plunge into the ocean of bountiful spiritual knowledge and training to become a Taoist master.

"Kind prince, true masters are the embodiment of heavenly energy. They are the direct expression of Tao. They must have attained spiritual maturity through true life experience in the world. Then they can become the spiritual light to those in darkness. To be with them is to experience the living truth. Their minds are as deep and all-encompassing as the Tao. By breaking through the mystery of life and death and the dreamlike quality of their own mental faculty they have fully developed and integrated all aspects of their being, and their personal nature is one with Tao. Their speech and behavior are the manifestation of their own spiritual attainment, responding to the different personalities and environments they encounter. Their lives are an expression of wisdom and pure law. They are the revelation of the mystery of the great universal triad: Heaven, Earth, and Man. Their smiles radiate light, wisdom, and bliss. They teach others selflessly, not out of any desire for self-aggrandizement. They are the true father and mother, true brother and sister, and true friend of their disciples. Their grace always illuminates the dark corners of the disciples' minds.

They share their divine energy with their disciples and are always aware of their problems. They dissolve their disciples' pain in the ocean of their compassion. The sadness, imperfection, and false personalities of the disciples vanish before their eyes and they see only the disciples' true nature.

"Because they know the traps and obstacles of life, they can guide their disciples out of troubled waters. The trials they give their disciples are a process of strengthening and building. They sometimes scold their disciples in an attempt to awaken them; if a disciple misunderstands this, loses faith, and gives up everything, it means he has fallen from the spiritual path and failed himself. If a disciple is foolish enough to rely on his own cleverness, he will endlessly go around and around in the false illusions of his own ego.

"True masters can awaken the disciples' divine energy and lead them to enlightenment. They can direct the stream of their disciples' lives toward the infinite ocean of Tao. A good disciple humbly and gratefully accepts the master so that he or she can proceed directly on the true path of Tao. With love, gratitude, and sincerity, the disciple should be willing to dedicate his entire being to the master and his teaching, to respectfully accept the instructions of the master and faithfully follow, serve, and obey the master. If a disciple remains single-purposed and unwaivering in his self-cultivation, he will surely attain self-mastery and become qualified to guide others to do the same."

As the old master was about to conclude his dialogue, he inquired of the prince and all his disciples, "Kind prince and all of my beloved friends, I have talked a lot. Did I really say anything since you have been with me? My dear disciples, since I started my journey to the West I have not said one thing. The subtle truth cannot be concluded in words. What all of you have listened to is the eternal breath of Tao which has been emanating through me and all of you. The subtle voice of the universal origin has been speaking since the beginning of the universe. To those whose energy can respond to it, this sound is very distinct. To those whose energy cannot respond to it, the sound is muffled and obscure. The subtle melody of universal life is eternal and constant, yet only those who are in consonance with it can perceive it.

"Kind prince, listen only to one who speaks with life. Obey that law which is so subtle it cannot be written. Follow only the one who does not show himself. Worship the unformed, embrace the unnamed, and unite yourself with what is not entrapped by any form that existed before Heaven, Earth, or Man. Respect the one who makes no demands. Say what cannot be said in words. Have intercourse with the subtle. Offer unconditional love to all life and trust the invariable, positive nature of the universe.

"My beloved disciples, an integral being never comes and goes. The voice of the Integral One will always be with you! Always listen for the nonverbal voice and you will reach the Divine Origin. When all words are exhausted, the truth appears.

"Be happy and content with your integral nature, for this is where we can meet and embrace each other and be together eternally. Never be bewildered by any transitory phenomena. Steadfastly keep pace with the subtle, eternal, divine energy within and without."

The master finished his dialogue, and the audience, both beings and nonbeings, greatly rejoiced at having had the opportunity to learn the Universal Way. They sincerely accepted and cherished the teaching and maintained it as the only true guidance in their lives. They practiced their virtue and refined themselves while living in the world. A healthy, natural life was their standard of living. Their work was an expression of their virtue and a reward for their creative minds and hands. They maintained balance and harmony as the essential principles of their lives. They followed the integral truth of the universe and were not inclined to follow any partial doctrine. They chose the fellowship of integral truth as the unified expression of their spiritual vantage point.

Periodic retreat from society was their renaissance, yet they did not use their retreat as an excuse for inertia or as an escape from their spiritual obligation to awaken and purify the world. They realized that a normal, balanced life is much more important than full-time retreat. They lived and worked in the world without being affected by it. They maintained themselves as contemplative hermits without the need to withdraw from the world and become self-enclosed. They quietly continued the divine spiritual mission by making the natural, spiritual, traditional education available to all people in any generation; following the describable to cultivate the indescribable, performing that which can be spoken of in order to arrive at that which cannot be spoken of. Many of them accomplished their worldly mission and inner evolution, and spiritually ascended to the divine realms in broad daylight with their physical lives. Those indestructible universal souls, whether returning to the physical world again as human beings or enjoying the subtle realm eternally, are the true essence of universal life. It is they who continue to inspire the precious truths of the universe in their human disciples in order to preserve the sacred teaching of the Universal Way as the true guidance for all natural lives."

About the Author

Hua-Ching Ni is an author, teacher, and physician who addresses the essential nature of human life and assists people with their personal growth and development. Having been raised in a long family tradition of healing and spirituality, Hua-Ching Ni spent his youth learning from highly achieved masters in the mountains of China. He is the beneficiary of a broad spiritual tradition passed down since the golden age of China.

Hua-Ching Ni writes in Chinese and English on ancient philosophy, Integral medicine, acupuncture and herbology, spiritual cultivation, Chinese astrology, Tai Chi Chuan, Chi Gong, meditation, and related subjects. His writing springs from his life experience, teaching, and spiritual development as well as his practice of Chinese medicine and acupuncture spanning over half a century in China and the West. Master Ni is also the chancellor of Yo San University of Traditional Chinese Medicine in Santa Monica, California. He has lectured worldwide on religion, philosophy, and special practices for building a natural healthy life and the cultivation of spiritual growth.

For more information about Master Ni's work, please contact:

SevenStar Communications
1314 Second Street
Santa Monica, CA 90401

Printed in the United States
by Baker & Taylor Publisher Services